William Denton

The Christians of Turkey

Their condition under Mussulman rule

William Denton

The Christians of Turkey
Their condition under Mussulman rule

ISBN/EAN: 9783337290542

Printed in Europe, USA, Canada, Australia, Japan

Cover: Foto ©ninafisch / pixelio.de

More available books at **www.hansebooks.com**

THE CHRISTIANS OF TURKEY

THEIR CONDITION UNDER

MUSSULMAN RULE

By REV. W. DENTON, M.A.

AUTHOR OF 'SERVIA AND THE SERVIANS,'
ETC. ETC.

LONDON
DALDY, ISBISTER & CO.
56, LUDGATE HILL
1876

[*The right of Translation is reserved.*]

INTRODUCTION.

THIRTEEN years ago, under the title of 'The Christians in Turkey,' I published a pamphlet, the greater part of which I am about to reprint in the present volume. Unhappily the description which I gave so many years ago of the state and condition of the Christian subjects of Turkey is as applicable at the present time as it was then. In 1863 the minds of the people of England were unprepared to believe that the position of our brethren in that empire was so miserable as they now know it to be, and my pamphlet excited but little attention. I have now, however, been asked by some of those who read it when first printed to allow of its republication, and I respond to that request by embodying the information, sad and harrowing as it is, in the present volume. I have made but few alterations in the parts republished. Some mere temporary references have been omitted, and some few illustrations have been added, and in addition I have devoted one chapter to a brief survey of the different races which occupy the European provinces of Turkey, and another to tracing the cause for the outbreak in the Herzegovina which was the herald of the present war between Servia and Montenegro with the Porte. Beyond these additions this volume is mainly a reprint of the pamphlet of thirteen years ago: thirteen years of grave responsibility to us: thirteen years of violated promises on the part of the Turkish Government: thirteen years of intense misery and suffering, of violence and of massacre, for the Christian subjects of Turkey.

I refer to the length of time which has gone by since the original publication of 'The Christians in Turkey,' and to the fact that the survey of the condition of these people is in the main reprinted from that pamphlet, to remove any misconception of my motive in putting forth the present volume. I have no wish to seem even to serve the interests or passions of party. I make no charge against any one set of ministers of state. To do so would be dishonest. The picture which I here reproduce of Turkish rule will at least show that the Ministry of the present day is not more responsible for the evils which weigh so heavily upon our Christian brethren in Turkey than former administrations. Any words of blame on my part are directed against that 'foreign policy' which has been pursued more or less consistently since the beginning of the Crimean war. I prefer therefore to alter the language of my former publication as little as possible, though some words and references may have but little applicability to the present. There has, however, been no change of circumstance, at least no amelioration in the condition of the Christians of Turkey, but the reverse. Their lot is harder, their condition more intolerable, in proportion to the decline in strength and number of the dominant race.

If, indeed, this question were one of mere party politics, I should not venture to intrude into a region where the presence of a clergyman is rightly regarded as incongruous. It is because the unhappy circumstances which surround so many millions of our brethren inhabiting some of the fairest and most fertile portions of the globe, ought not to awaken party animosities, that I ask the attention of the reader to a review of the present wrongs of the Christians in Turkey, in order, not indeed to enlist the sympathies of Englishmen in their behalf, for this they already have, but to give to these sympathies a definite direction. Indeed, with rare and noble exceptions, it must be confessed that party politicians of all shades of opinion are almost equally uninformed on this subject, and therefore equally indifferent to the sufferings of the great mass of the people of Turkey. This fact, whilst it removes this great political question out of the arena of party strife, at the same time renders more difficult the attempt to obtain for it an attentive hearing from those who seek, or affect to guide, popular opinion. My object, let me state at the outset, is to ask that our governors should cease from that strange interference against the people of Turkey which has been for some years the policy of the English Government, and that they should no longer actively aid a despotism the most grinding on the face of the earth : one which, not content with the fanatical cruelty which led to the Diocletian and other early persecutions, poisons and pollutes the whole domestic life of the vast majority of the subjects of Turkey.

There is another reason why I prefer to reproduce my former words. In the indignation felt and expressed throughout all England there lurks one danger. In dwelling upon the atrocities perpetrated in Bulgaria we may come to believe that these were exceptional in their character, an outbreak caused by some momentary panic, or by a sudden uncontrollable frenzy which may possibly never again occur. This is not true. They do but illustrate the normal condition of the provinces of Turkey. What has happened in Bulgaria has happened also in Bosnia. Deeds have been done there as horrible as those done in Bulgaria, even if the number of victims should fall short of those in the latter province. Only by what may almost be called an accident were the atrocities perpetrated at Batak and elsewhere unveiled to us. We were made acquainted with one set of facts, we are in ignorance as to the extent of the other atrocities. Our ignorance indeed is our only excuse for the continuance of such horrors.

In a letter written by an English gentleman resident at Constantinople, and quoted by Mr Cobden in a debate in the House of Commons in 1863, the following passage occurs:—' What is our policy supporting? Some one asked me how to account for this in a people the most moral of all, the English, that these deepest immoralities should be maintained by their patronage? I replied, they are, for the most part, quite ignorant, or unwilling to believe what they hear.' When that ignorance is removed, when they know what is really meant by the phrase 'supporting the integrity of Turkey,' Englishmen,

I am assured, will no longer sustain by their patronage a Government which exists only to inflict misery upon its subjects, whether by its active oppression or by its helplessness and imbecility.

That this ignorance on the part of the people of England should exist is not to be wondered at. The same ignorance as to the condition of the people of Turkey, and of the habits and feelings of the large Christian communities which cover the face of that empire, has been long shared in by successive Governments in this country. The broad distinction, however, between the ignorance of the people of England and that of the Government, lies in the circumstance that the latter has always had it in its power to obtain information, from which it has intentionally turned away, and has even taken considerable pains to suppress, whilst the ignorance of the people of England arises from the deliberate action of their governors in preventing, so far as possible, any information reaching this country as to the real condition of the people of Turkey. Since the time of Sir Henry Bulwer the large consular staff scattered throughout the dominions of the Sultan, either by positive instructions, or by those indirect means by which men are made acquainted with the wishes of their superiors, have long known

INTRODUCTION.

that amongst the most important duties which the Government required them to perform is a complete withholding all information as to the state, and especially as to the sufferings, of the people of Turkey. They are bidden significantly to shut their eyes, even if they cannot harden their hearts, against the daily recurring atrocities practised upon the unarmed and wretched peasantry of Roumelia, of Asia Minor, and of Syria, so that in answer to interrogations in the House of Commons respecting any case of grievous wrong, it may be answered by the organ of the Foreign Office, that no account of any such occurrence has been received from the consul on the spot, and that therefore the presumption is that such report is untrue.

What the impression and the practice of the consuls in this matter is may be gathered from the following extract from a letter addressed to me by Dr Sandwith, well known as the Chief of the Medical staff during the siege of Kars:—

'When I was in Turkey, about two years ago, I had a long conversation with a consul, who told me stories that curdled my blood with horror concerning the cruelties and barbarities of the Turks, chiefly towards the Christians, but their misdeeds were by no means confined to the unbelievers. Wherever a pasha could plunder, he never cared what ruin and misery were the result. The consul showed me clearly how inevitably the country was being ruined and depopulated. "At all events," I remarked, "you have the satisfaction of reporting all these horrors in your despatches?" "Oh dear, no," he answered, "I dare not. We have received more than a hint that our Government is determined to uphold Turkey; and if I were to tell the truth, and describe things as they really are, my career would be ruined. More than one consul has been severely snubbed for doing so." On another occasion I heard also from a consular official of a horrible case of judicial torture. I asked for the details. He durst not give me them, and told me the case would not be reported, as the consuls had been made to understand that any reports unfavourable to the Turks would be unwelcome to the embassy.'

The experience of Dr Sandwith is borne out by that of many other travellers in the countries subject to the Sultan. English consuls who wish to stand well with the Embassy at Constantinople must make their reports as favourable as possible to Turkey, and conceal all facts which would enlighten

INTRODUCTION. 11

the English public as to the true nature of Turkish rule. Hence the long delay in informing the Government of the Bulgarian atrocities. Since the publication of my pamphlet additional evidence has been tendered me in confirmation of this statement, and I have obtained permission of Dr Manning, the secretary of the Religious Tract Society, the writer of the following letter, to print this confirmation of the words of Dr Sandwith already quoted:—

'SOME surprise and incredulity having been expressed as to your statements respecting the consular reports from Turkey, I think it due to you to say that my own observations fully confirm their accuracy. Travelling in Egypt, Syria, and Turkey in Europe a few years ago, the sufferings of the people under the brutal and stupid tyranny of the Turks filled me with indignation. The reply everywhere given to my inquiry why the facts were not made known in England was, that the consuls were expected to make their reports as favourable as possible to the Turkish Government, and that any report in a contrary sense would be regarded with disfavour at Constantinople.'

But on this matter we are not left to conjecture, or even to seek for the testimony of men of veracity.

It is witnessed to by the papers presented to Parliament. The following instance will illustrate this policy.

In the early part of 1860, Prince Gortschakoff, the Russian Minister for Foreign Affairs, addressed a circular to the Great Powers of Europe, pointing out the continuance of that injustice of which the Christians in Turkey had so long complained, and which the Porte had, at various periods, for upwards of thirty years, promised should be removed. In that circular, which was dated in May, 1860, the following statement occurs :—

'The attention which the discussions upon the condition of the East has excited throughout Europe, makes us desirous of freeing from all error and false and exaggerated interpretation the part which the Imperial Cabinet has taken, and the object which it proposes to itself in this matter.

'For more than a year the official reports of our agents in Turkey have made us acquainted with the increasingly serious condition of the Christian provinces under the rule of the Porte, and especially of Bosnia, Herzegovina, and Bulgaria. This condition does not date from to-day, but, far from getting

INTRODUCTION. 13

better, as was hoped, it has become worse during the last few years.

'In this conviction, after having, on the one hand, vainly sought to enlighten the Turkish Government on the gravity of the circumstances, by communicating to it successively all the accounts which have been made known to us of the abuses committed by local authorities; and after having, on the other hand, exhausted all means of persuasion that we could use among the Christians, in order to induce them to patience, we have frankly and loyally addressed ourselves to the Cabinets of the Great Powers of Europe. We have explained to them the circumstances, as described in the reports of our agents; the imminence of a crisis; our conviction that isolated representations, sterile or palliative promises, will no longer suffice as a preventive; and also the necessity of an understanding of the Great Powers among themselves and with the Porte, that they will consult together as to the measures which can alone put an end to this dangerous state of things. We have not made absolute propositions as to the course to be adopted. We have confined ourselves to showing the urgency, and indicating the object. As to the first, we have not concealed the fact that it appears to us to admit of no doubt, and to allow of no delay.

'First of all, an immediate local inquiry, with the participation of Imperial delegates, in order to verify the reality of the facts; next, an understanding which it is reserved for the Great Powers to establish with each other and with the Porte, in order to engage it to adopt the necessary organic measures for bringing about in its relations with the Christian populations of the empire, a real, serious, and durable amelioration.

'There is nothing here, then, in the shape of an interference wounding to the dignity of the Porte. We do not suspect its intentions; it is the Power most interested in a departure from the present situation. Be it the result of blindness, tolerance, or feebleness, the concurrence of Europe cannot but be useful to the Porte, whether to enlighten its judgment or to fortify its action. There can no longer be a question of an attack on its rights, which we desire to see respected, or of creating complications, which it is our wish to prevent. The understanding which we wish to see established between the Great Powers and the Turkish Government, must be to the Christians a proof that their fate is taken into consideration, and that we are seriously occupied in ameliorating it. At the same time, it will be to the Porte a certain pledge of the friendly intentions of the Powers which have placed the conservation of the Ottoman Empire among the essential conditions of the European equilibrium. Thus, both sides ought to see in it a motive: the Turkish Government, for confidence and security—the Christians, for patience and hope. Europe, on its part, after past experience, will not, in our opinion, find elsewhere than in this moral action the guarantees which a question of the first rank demands, with which its tranquillity is indissolubly connected, and in which the interests of humanity mingle with those of policy. Our August Master has never disavowed the strong sympathy with which the former inspire him. His Majesty desires not to burden his conscience with the reproach of having remained silent in the face of such sufferings, when so many voices are raised elsewhere, under circumstances much less imperious. We are, moreover, profoundly convinced that this order of ideas is inseparable from the political interest which Russia, like all the other Powers, has in the maintenance of the Ottoman Empire.

'We trust that these views are shared by all the Cabinets; but we are also convinced that the time for illusions is past, that any hesitation, any adjournment, will have grave consequences. In combining, with all our efforts, to place the Ottoman Government in a course which may avert these eventualities, we believe that we are giving it a proof of our solicitude, while at the same time we fulfil a duty to humanity.'

Upon the receipt of this circular, Sir H. Bulwer, acting under the instructions of the English Government, drew up a list of questions, which he sent to the various consuls throughout Turkey. No persons could, from their position, better speak on such a subject; none would be more ready to furnish evidence which would contradict the assertions of the Russian note, provided that this were possible. From their answer, honestly, faithfully, and intelligently given, we might have had a luminous survey of the Turkish empire. Such a report would have been invaluable. It was not likely that English consuls would exaggerate the unhappy condition of the Christians, since they had been made to feel in many ways that even truth on this subject was 'unwelcome to the embassy;' and before sending in their answers they were reminded that their very bread depended upon the will of his Excellency the Ambassador.* At the same time, it is evident, that

* 'I assure you that your conduct at this crisis will be

reports from the pens of English gentlemen, making allowances for this circumstance, would, on the whole, present a faithful picture of the condition of the people—slightly coloured, perhaps, in favour of things as they are, and framed in some degree to meet the wishes of the Government which they served, but still generally trustworthy. It would seem, however, that Sir Henry Bulwer felt, from the first, some misgivings that a simple answer to these questions would confirm every jot and tittle of the accusations of the Russian minister, and accordingly he took the unusual step of issuing a circular, dated 'Constantinople, June 11th, 1860,' and inclosing it under the same cover as the questions, by which circular he directed the consuls in what way he wished and expected them to answer the questions. In this circular, which one of the consuls rightly calls an 'instruction,' Sir Henry Bulwer said—

'Looking at the barbarous and despotic power but a few years since exercised by the Pashas in the Provinces, and at the venal practices too long indulged in by Turkish functionaries,—the temptation

duly watched by me, and my opinion respecting it, whether favourable or the reverse, communicated to Her Majesty's Government.'—*Circular of Sir H. Bulwer to Her Majesty's Consuls, August* 8, 1860.

being not unoften given by the Rayahs themselves, who bribed such functionaries to favour the one against the other,—it is too much to expect that a pure and perfect administration will now be found.

'The crimes, moreover, signalized by Russia, are in all countries unfortunately to be seen and deplored; and whilst religious toleration, to a far greater extent than is even now practised by many European Governments, has been traditionally characteristic of Turkish domination,—a system of religious equality, though by no means easy to establish at first—when the conquering race is of one creed, and the conquered of another,—has, nevertheless, of late years, made a visible progress in the capital; and can hardly, one would suppose, since it has been proclaimed ostentatiously and constantly, with the consent of the Sovereign, be altogether disregarded by the Porte's official servants in the country at large.

'Thus,—whilst I am far from denying that great and radical reforms are required in the provincial administration, I am, nevertheless, inclined to believe that it is an exaggeration to contend that things are in a *much* worse state than under the circumstances might be expected, or that there is a constant and perverse action, on the part of the Governors and their subordinates, in opposition to the general policy which their superiors are pledged to carry out.'

And Sir Henry Bulwer then significantly added—

'Her Majesty's Government wishes, as you well know, to maintain the Ottoman Empire,—which in its fall would produce a general disorganization in the East, accompanied, probably, by war throughout the world,—the whole producing a series of disasters which would certainly not benefit any class in Turkey, and would be likely to cause great calamities to mankind.'

Now it is evident that had Sir Henry Bulwer believed that the state of Turkey was improved or improving, he might have safely left it to the consuls to make such a declaration without telling them that he expected them to do so. If under the mild 'toleration' of Turkey the Christians were reposing in peace and were free from grievous oppressions, it was not necessary that the ambassador at Constantinople should tell this to the consuls, who must have known far better than he could what was the condition of the Christians. That his circular was regarded by the consuls as a dictation as to the kind of answers desired by Sir Henry Bulwer, and 'welcome to the

Embassy,' is evident from a circumstance which, if it were not for the gravity of the offence against the very first principles of morality, would be simply ludicrous. By some mistake in the office of the ambassador, the list of questions was received by one consul without the circular which should have accompanied it; on the 4th of August, that gentleman forwarded his answers in simple child-like faith that his Excellency required truthful answers to his questions. A few days, however, after the report had been sent, the circular arrived under another cover. It was then evident to him that he had committed a great blunder; he had been asked to bless the Sultan, to praise his beneficent and 'tolerant' rule, and to contradict the accusation in the Russian note. Alas! he had unwittingly cursed the one and confirmed the other by a simple picture of the state of the province in which he resided. Here it would obviously have been better to have let the matter rest, the mistake of not sending the questions and the draught answers together had been made at Constantinople, and the blunder of telling the truth had been solely committed in consequence of the first error. This, however, did not satisfy the consul. He did what terrified men frequently do. He was bold even to rashness. He undertook to confute himself, and wrote a despatch full of lamentation at his simplicity, and overflowing with apologies for speaking the truth. In this latter document the consul professes that he is not so competent to speak as his Excellency, his ideas are all 'crude,' and he seeks to recall his former statement, seemingly not knowing it was too late to do so. Eating his leek with a very wry face, in his alarm he made a larger meal of it than was at all necessary.

In his second report, written after he had learnt why Sir Henry Bulwer had sent the list of questions to him, the consul thus writes—

'On the 4th instant I had the honour of forwarding my replies to the queries contained in your Excellency's circular of June 11, which had reached me only a few days previously, and yesterday I received the other circular bearing the same date. I thus furnished what information I could *without being aware of the motives dictating the questions, and without being in possession of the valuable instructions conveyed by the other circular.* I shall, therefore, endeavour now to supply the deficiencies of my replies.

* * * * *

'Your Excellency expresses the belief that it is an exaggeration to contend that things are in a *much worse state* than, under the circumstances, might be expected. This view of the case is fully corroborated by my experience.

* * * * *

'I am sure your Excellency wishes to have opinions frankly stated, in order that they may be duly sifted, and appreciated according to their merits and demerits; and I therefore hope I may be held excused if I have too freely given utterance to these crude notions on a subject, the consideration of which may not strictly form part of a consul's attributes.'

It is a melancholy spectacle to see a man of mature age making piteous appeals for tender consideration because he had unfortunately spoken the truth; but however melancholy the spectacle is, it is important, since it shows us the effect of the circular of Sir Henry Bulwer upon the mind at least of one of the consuls, and it leaves us to regret that we have missed those valuable photographs of the state of Turkey which, but for the forethought of Sir Henry Bulwer, we should have obtained. Under the circumstances, therefore, every admission of the consular body as to the misrule, the oppression, and cruelty practised by the officers of the Turkish Government, acquires additional weight. Nor would it be right to pass over, without a word of admiration, the courage which has led some of those officers to speak plain words and to declare unpalatable truths in their reports.

But the record of the freaks of British diplomacy are not at an end. The papers lately presented to Parliament are full of mournful instances of the way in which truth is paltered with, equivocation resorted to, and even positive untruth suggested, when it is thought necessary to throw the shield of England's might—I wish I could say England's greatness—over the cruel oppression and the profligate sensuality of Turkey. I will not weary the reader by quoting, as I might, the numerous despatches of Sir Henry Bulwer, especially those which occur in the Blue Books on the Syrian massacres, which illustrate this dishonesty.

By means, then, such as these—the systematic suppression of information, and the requiring our consular agents to make one-sided, partial, and coloured statements—are the sympathies of the public of this country diverted from the sufferings of the people of the East. But, let us bear in mind, in our zeal to preserve, at all hazards, 'the integrity of Turkey,' that the integrity of our public men is greatly suffering, and the honour and humanity of England are in danger of becoming bywords in many parts of the world. It would surely be more manly, more honourable, more politic, to grapple with the real facts of the case. It would be better—for honesty is still the best policy—to acknowledge that though the Government of Turkey is hopelessly dead or dying; though the moral corruption of all classes in that country, but especially of its rulers, has reached such a stage that it is too polluting a subject to be even mentioned, still less detailed; though the unhappy subject races are exposed to daily massacres and to outrages worse than death; though portions of the empire, naturally amongst the most fertile on the globe—tracts of land which a few years ago were cultivated with the same care as the gardens of Flanders or of Lombardy—are now a waste wilderness, trodden only by the feet of wandering Bedouins, by some Christian flying from the intolerable oppression of his savage masters, or, more commonly, only by prowling beasts of prey, for this —as I shall be able to show from documents of unimpeachable veracity—is, in brief, the condition of the greater part of Turkey in Asia—yet that in despite of all this it is for some reason or another so important to England to maintain all these abominations that we are resolved to do so. It would be better to acknowledge this: but not at the cost of our own 'integrity' to attempt to conceal that which is notoriously and unhappily true. We might still plead, if we would, that, all this accumulated misery and evil notwithstanding, it is sound policy to perpetuate these horrors, to sustain this crumbling pillar and to prop this falling edifice of Ottoman power. I confess that both humanity and policy are, in my opinion, damaged by the course which the Foreign Office is bent on pursuing; but, at any rate, if necessary, let that course be held to without resorting to equivocation, deceit, and falsehood. Such weapons indicate a desperate cause, or they will injure that which, but for their use, need not be despaired of.

I shall abstain as much as possible from any evidence or conclusions of my own. I have an abundance of witnesses whom I can cite, and I prefer their testimony to any which I can bring as to the condition of the great bulk of the people of Turkey. The witnesses whom I am about to quote are for the most part our own consuls settled in that country. These write with an evident consciousness that any bias in favour of the oppressed races of that country would be 'unwelcome to the Embassy,' and, as Sir Henry Bulwer had informed them in writing before requiring their testimony, to the British Government itself, yet they testify to these facts :—

(I.) That the most fertile provinces in Turkey, formerly and even recently covered with flourishing villages and occupied by industrious inhabitants, are now waste and desolate, filled only with ruin, the mouldering remains of slaughtered men and children, and with prowling beasts of prey. That the former inhabitants have been massacred or driven away, and that the sands of the desert are fast encroaching upon what were formerly the most fruitful lands on the globe.

(II.) That moral corruption the most horrible, and sensuality the most loathsome, has become *universal* amongst the Turkish people, and is fast depopulating the empire and destroying the whole Mussulman race.

(III.) That alarm and terror for the lives and honour of their families reign in every quarter of the Turkish empire. That there is no security for industry, no safety for life; and that with the diminution of the dominant race, the jealousy and hatred of the Turk towards the Christian is acquiring fresh force.

(IV.) That no attempt has been made by the Turkish Government to fulfil the engagements which, from time to time, it has entered into with the Great Powers of Europe to guard against the oppression of the subject race.

(V.) That in the Christian races of Turkey, and in them only, are there any signs of life, and that their rapid increase in numbers and material prosperity, as well as the extension of education amongst them, together with their superior industry and morality, afford the only hope for the future.

That the condition of the people of Turkey—the large mass of the population of that country—presents the sad spectacle which I have here indicated, and which I am about to illustrate from official and other unexceptionable documents, I believe no one at all acquainted with the subject will deny. The utmost that the apologists of Turkey are accustomed to plead is, that the depopulation, the massacres, the cruel acts of injustice practised toward the Christians, arise not from the direct action of the Turkish Government, but from the corruption of the officers and the fanaticism of the Mussulmans, which it is too feeble to restrain or punish. This, no doubt, is in part true; but then it ought to be remembered that the very feebleness of the central Government arises from its injustice. But, indeed, this is only true in part. The men who compose the Turkish Government—the owners of the sumptuous palaces which fringe the Bosphorus, are in no degree removed above the crowd in intelligence, in uprightness, or in morality; and much of the ruin which lies like a heavy blight on the land, and the present hopeless condition of the Ottoman empire, arise from the positive sins of its Government, its miserable faithlessness towards its subjects, as well as from its inherent powerlessness.

Practically, however, it is of little consequence to men who suffer, to what quarter the source of the evil of which they complain may be traced. A peasant who is stripped of his property because he is a Christian—whose testimony in a court of justice is refused for the same reason—who has been arbitrarily imprisoned—whose wife and daughter have been outraged, and whose sons have been executed because they ventured to defend the honour of their mother and sisters—derives no comfort from being told that all these things have happened, not from the vice and corruption of the Government, but only from its weakness or its want of power to protect him. And let it be remembered, that every means which statecraft can devise — protocols without number, alliances on all sides, conventions to avoid wars, and wars which have happened notwithstanding—have all been resorted to with the view of infusing new life into the veins of that dying body, and to give it artificial strength, but all without avail. The ruin goes on at an accelerated speed-- the feeble Government is becoming every day more hopelessly feeble.

CHAPTER I.

POPULATION OF TURKEY.

THE races which occupy the country between the Danube and the Bosphorus—not taking account of Greece, which was erected some fifty years since into an independent kingdom; Montenegro, which has never submitted to the yoke of the Ottoman; and the principalities of Roumania and Servia, which are autonomous, and virtually independent—are the Bulgarians, the Serbs, the Albanians, and the Greeks. These are placed in the order of their numerical importance. It is not an easy matter to obtain correct statistics of the Turkish people among whom they live, and in some instances, it may be, the number of the Christians is somewhat understated. It is believed, however, that the statistics here given will be found pretty correct. In some instances they are obtained from official returns.

POPULATION OF TURKEY. 31

The Bulgarians	4,540,000
The Serbs of Bosnia, Herzegovina, etc.	2,030,000
The Albanians	1,150,000
The Greeks outside of the kingdom of Greece	1,048,700

Add to these—

| Armenians, Georgians, etc. | 420,000 |
| Wallachians not living in Wallachia | 225,000 |

Total . . 9,543,700

There are about 80,000 Jews living in the cities in the southern part of European Turkey, and more than double that number of Gipsies (165,000), who wander throughout the whole country, whether autonomous or subject. The Circassians are estimated at 144,000. The Turkish element of the population of European Turkey, excluding those living in Roumania, may be estimated at about 1,260,000; according to the most liberal calculation, 1,326,000; but this errs, if at all, on the side of too large an amount. The numbers of the Turkish race also are in a rapid state of decline in every province of European Turkey.*

Though the Bulgarians, the Serbs, and the Greeks have, in the face of long and severe persecution, for the most part, maintained their faith in Christ, yet large numbers have at various times—chiefly in past years—apostatized from their belief; though many, it is thought, have only conformed outwardly to Mahomedanism to avoid the sufferings of their Christian brethren, or for the sake of worldly advantage. For this reason the numbers of the Turks and non-Mussulman population are not identical with the Christians and Mahometans. According to race the relative proportion of Turks and non-Turks may be thus stated:—

  Non-Turkish races 11,583,700
  Turks 1,260,000

Estimated, however, according to their religion, the people of European Turkey are:—

---

* The official figures communicated to the editor of the Saxe-Gotha Almanack gives 2,095,833 as the *estimated* number of the Turkish population; but to make up so large a Turkish population the Armenian Christians—who number, according to the most trustworthy information, 420,000, the largest number of whom inhabit Pera, Constantinople, and Adrianople—and also the Gipsies, are included with the Turks!

POPULATION OF TURKEY. 33

Christian . 10,673,700
Mahometan 2,200,000

I believe that both these figures, the estimated number of Turks in the one case and of Mahometans in the other, are in excess of the real amount of the Turkish and Mussulman element in the population.

Reckoning the Serbs of the principality of Servia and the people of Roumania, or the Danubian principality, the Turkish element is relatively small. As, however, these states are virtually free, and contain scarcely any Mussulmans, the Christians and Mahometans in the provinces ruled directly from Constantinople are more nearly balanced in point of numbers, although even here the Christian element largely preponderates. The population of Servia and Roumania, the latter principality of which contains 1300 Mussulmans, is estimated at—

Roumania 4,500,000
Servia . 1,340,000

In both cases the population is an increasing one. As the large and constant decline of the Turkish population is due mainly to the corruption of morals throughout the empire, we have in the steady increase of the Christian races, especially when their numbers are not kept down by the massacres which take place, an answer to the charge sometimes made against them, that, granted the Turkish part of the population is given over to vices which destroy it, yet the Christians are as bad, or at least are almost as bad, as the Mussulmans. The decline in the one case and the steady increase in numbers in the other is a vindication of the Christian race in this respect.

Bulgaria is not the only home of the Bulgarian people. As in the case of Servia, the territory is more limited than the race. As the Serbs occupy Bosnia, Herzegovina, and Old Servia, as well as the principality of that name, so the Bulgarian people not only inhabit the province of Bulgaria, but make up a considerable part of the population of Thrace, Macedonia, Thessaly, and even Albania. Originally a Tartar race, and not dissimilar to the Turks at their first appearance in history, the Bulgarians crossed the Danube and settled on the north of the Balkan mountains in the seventh century. In the ninth century they embraced Christianity, and for awhile were the ruling power on the southern borders of the Danube. They were conquered, however, and incorporated in the Servian monarchy of Stephen Dushan, and from similarity of origin, of language, and of identity in religion, became what they now are, virtually a Sclavonic people. The old kingdom of

Bulgaria came to an end in 1390, when the people submitted to the Turks, on the condition that they should be allowed to govern themselves and merely pay a tribute to the Sultan. These terms, however, were gradually set aside, and every vestige of their liberty was destroyed. Mr Paton, writing twenty years ago, says, 'They are a most unwarlike race, and submissive to the Turks as sheep to a colley dog. Their habits are pastoral and agricultural, having neither the soldier spirit and gigantic stature of the Serb, nor the mercantile enterprise and intelligence of the Greek.'* They are distinguished for their industry, honesty, domestic virtue, and submissiveness. Recently a great awakening to the advantage of education has taken place, and almost every village has its school, supported by a rate voluntarily paid by the inhabitants. In the towns which I have visited their schools are large, well built, and supplied with good school apparatus. The numbers of the Bulgarians are estimated at 4,500,000, though some think that their true number is nearer 6,000,000. Those who live in the province of Bulgaria are stated on Turkish official authority to amount to 1,837,053.

* The Danube and Adriatic, by A. A. Paton, vol. i. pp. 292, 293.

The Serbs of Turkey, as distinguished from the people of Sclavonia and Austrian Croatia,* occupy the provinces of Bosnia and Herzegovina, the principality of Servia, and a tract on the south-west of that State known by the name of Old Servia. The Serbs of Servia proper submitted to the Turkish rule, at least in part, after the fatal battle of Kossova in 1389, and became a province of the empire in 1459. In 1804 the Servians revolted, and, under the leadership of Kara George, for nine years struggled against the authority of the Porte. In 1813 the Turks overcame this revolt, but in 1815 Milosh Obrenovich raised again the standard of independence, and after several vicissitudes the freedom of Servia was guaranteed by a Hatti Scheriff of the Sultan in 1830. Since that time Servia has been virtually free; by Firman of the Porte no Turkish subject is allowed to live within the limits of the principality, and a small tribute alone marks the suzerainty of the Porte. The population of the principality is, according to an official return, 1,338,505.†

Bosnia and *Herzegovina* surrendered to the Sultan

* The Sclavs of Austria, Tchecs, Slovacs, Serbs, and other kindred people, number nearly 20,000,000.
† Almanack de Gotha, 1875.

of Turkey in the year 1454. In these provinces the large landowners, with hardly an exception, apostatized to Mahometanism, and by so doing retained their possessions and feudal privileges. The bulk of the population, however, remained Christians. These are divided into two sections,—members of the Orthodox or Eastern Church, and members of the Roman Catholic Church. According to the official report of 1874, the total population of this province, for Herzegovina is included in the Vilajet of Bosnia, was as follows:—

Greek Christians 576,756
Roman Catholics 185,503
Mussulmans (Bosniac, not Turkish) . 442,050
Jews 3,000
Gipsies 9,537

Total . 1,216,846

In this tripartite division of the Serb population consists the difficulty of forming an autonomous government for these two provinces. But this is a difficulty as great at the present moment as it can be in a period of autonomy. Whilst the Bosniac beys, with those of Herzegovina, are fanatical Mussulmans, they are as fanatically anti-Turk; and it would probably be easier to combine them under one rule as an independent State, notwithstanding religious differences, than it has been to overcome the antipathy of race between the people, of whatever race they may be, and their Osmanli rulers, the Turks of Constantinople. Indeed the Turkish Court now holds a precarious rule over these provinces, only by playing off religion against religion. The members of the Latin Church are in these provinces invested with peculiar privileges which are withheld from the members of the Orthodox or Eastern Church. The whole modern history of Bosnia has been a series of insurrections, mostly of the Mussulman aristocracy against the Turkish officials and the authority of the Porte.

Montenegro has always maintained its independence of Turkey, and though it has received tempting offers of an increase of territory on condition of its acknowledging the suzerainty of the Porte, it has always rejected the offer. Its population is estimated at about 200,000.

The *Albanians*, divided into different clans, and generally supposed to be the descendants of the old Illyrian inhabitants driven southward by the inroads of the Sclavs, inhabit a rugged country, and this and their neighbourhood to the Montenegrins have enabled them to maintain a sort of turbulent independence. According to the official information of the Turkish Government, the population of these tribes is stated to be 1,245,182. Of them 750,000 are Christians of the Orthodox or of the Roman rite, and the rest Mahometans.

The whole of the possession of Turkey in Europe subject immediately to the Porte is divided into eight vilayets, or governments, each presided over by a Pasha. Constantinople is not included in these, having as its chief the Minister of Police.

CHAPTER II.

THE DECAY OF TURKEY.

THE first point which I indicated in my prefatory remarks as symptomatic of the decay and approaching extinction of Turkey is the desolation which is to be met with in all the provinces of the empire, and which is increasing in intensity, and widening in area. That this is so, we know from testimony which is as unimpeachable as it is uniform. The evidence is so abundant, and the witnesses to this fact so numerous, that the only difficulty arises from the necessity of selection.

Of the country about Smyrna, Mr Senior thus describes what met his own eye, and was pointed out to him by the Prussian consul:—'"A strong proof of the depopulation of the country is the presence of nomadic tribes, Irooks and Turcomans, who wander over it in parties of from thirty to forty families, carrying with them cattle, camels, horses, and sheep in thousands, encamping and feeding on the unoccupied lands. The Irooks live in tents; and, besides their pastoral employments, weave carpets and coarse cloths. The Turcomans are purely pastoral, and sometimes build temporary villages of wood coated with mud. I remember finding one near Sardis on the same spot for two successive years. They had 150 camels, 400 or 500 head of cattle, and perhaps 10,000 sheep. I asked them how long they intended to remain there. 'God only knows,' they answered. The next year they were gone."

' "To whom then," I said, "does the land on which they encamp, and feed their herds and flocks, belong?"

' "To the Sultan in general," he answered.

' " And do they pay for its use?"

' " Not," he replied, " when it is the Sultan's. The unoccupied land of the Sultan may be used without payment; when they use that belonging to private persons, some payment is exacted. They ought to pay tithe, but the appearance of a tithe-collector is a notice to them to depart."

' "How much of Asia Minor," I said, "do you suppose to be uncultivated?"

' "Ninety-nine hundredths," he answered; "if

you go from hence,towards Magnesia, you will ride ten hours through fine land without seeing a human habitation. But such is the fertility of the hundredth part which is cultivated, that if there were roads its produce would influence sensibly the markets of Europe."' *

Of the whole province of Palestine, Mr Finn, Her Majesty's Consul at Jerusalem, reported, that it is 'seriously under-populated, and consequently large tracts lie waste;' and of the inhabitants he writes:—'We have a thinly scattered population, almost entirely engaged in rural occupations, propagated like wild animals, without education, in the common acceptation of that word, or even a decent sense of any religion whatever, and ignorant of everything but the use of very clumsy fire-arms, and actuated by no conscientious feeling beyond the requirements of their clan or faction.' †

As to Aleppo and its neighbourhood, Mr Skene thus writes:—'This province is in a good condition as regards the amount of production. But unfor-

* A Journal kept in Turkey and Greece, by Nassau W. Senior, Esq. London: 1859.
† Report of Consuls on Condition of Christians in Turkey, p. 27.

tunately, the productive class does not enjoy in peace the fruits of labour. A portion of its produce is carried off by the nomadic Arabs, and extorted from the peasantry by the farmers of the tithes.

'Vast plains of the most fertile land lie waste on account of the incursions of the Bedouins, who drive the agricultural population westward, in order to secure pasture for their increasing flocks of sheep and herds of camels. I have seen twenty-five villages plundered by a single incursion of Sheik Mohammed Dukhy with 2000 Beni Sachar horsemen. I have visited a fertile district which possessed 100 villages twenty years ago, and found only a few lingering fellows, destined soon to follow their kindred to the hills ranging along the seaboard. I have explored towns in the Desert, with well-paved streets, houses still roofed, and their stone doors swinging on the hinges, ready to be occupied, and yet quite untenanted; thousands of acres of fine arable land spreading around them, with tracks of watercourses for irrigation, now yielding but a scanty pasture to the sheep and camels of the Bedouin. This overlapping of the Desert on the cultivated plains commenced eighty years ago, when the Anazi tribes migrated from Central Arabia in search of more extended pasturage, and overran Syria. It has now reached the sea on two points, near Acre, and between Latakia and Tripoli.

'The Arab, however, does not always carry off the whole stock of the villager, but is frequently satisfied by a conciliatory offering in money and grain. Something is thus left for extortion by the tax-gatherer. His operations are conducted in an equally open manner with those of the nomadic plunderer. When the tithes are put up to auction, the members of the Provincial Council select the villages whose revenues they wish to farm under the name of a retainer. They agree not to compete with each other, and use their joint endeavours to prevent others from outbidding them. When the highest price is offered the Pasha consults the Council, which declares it to be the full value; and a profitable bargain is obtained by the Councillor whose turn has come. Then begins the pressure on the villager. His grain is threshed and ready for sale, but he must not move it until the tithe is taken by the farmer. Prices are falling in the market with the daily increasing abundance. He implores permission to sell, and receives it only on consenting to double or treble the tax. In lieu of 10 per cent., there are instances of 40 per cent. being thus wrung from him, when the want of the necessaries of life for his family prevents his waiting longer. The peasant is next forced to convey the collector's share to town without remuneration, to feed his numerous satellites, to bring him presents of poultry, lambs, and forage, which latter produce is not tithed. He has no means of redress, for the voice of the all-powerful Council drowns every complaint. The Pasha is appealed to, and shrugs his shoulders.

'Still the agricultural population is not plunged in that hopeless state of destitution which might be expected under these conditions: so rich is the soil, so industrious and frugal the labourer.

'In the towns, until quite lately, trade and manufacturers were in a flourishing state. Since the revival, however, of the old feelings of aversion and animosity between the Mussulman and Christian communities, a disadvantageous change has consequently become apparent also in the material circumstances of the population. Want of confidence in the future is withdrawing capital from circulation; trade stagnates; and one-half of the looms previously worked are now at rest.'*

Of the province of Erzeroom, 'containing about

* Report of Consuls on Condition of Christians in Turkey, pp. 48, 49.

fifteen hundred villages,' we read :—'A correct census, I believe, is not desired by the Turks, who are conscious of a very sensible decrease in the Mussulman population in many provinces, and naturally would not like to publish this fact.'*

In Mr Senior's diary, again, occurs the following picture of the depopulation which is going on in Armenia: †—'*Saturday, October* 24*th.*—I sat at dinner next to V. W., who has just returned from the frontier separating Turkish and Russian Armenia.

'He gave a frightful account of the misgovernment of Turkish Armenia.

'"It is such," he said, "that the people are wishing for the Russians. A new Pasha—and there is one every three or four years—sends word of his arrival to all the subordinate local officers. This is a notice to all office-holders to be prepared with their bribes, and to all office-hunters to be prepared to outbribe them."

'"And how," I said, "do those who have bribed him get back their money?"

'"By increasing the taxation," he answered, "by not accounting for the public receipts, by wink-

* Narrative of the Siege of Kars. By Humphry Sandwith, M. D. London, 1856. P. 60.
† Senior, pp. 138-9.

ing at breaches of quarantine laws, or non-payment of custom-house dues, by selling justice, and through the *corres*. The last is a fertile source of profit. The Pasha is making a progress; the villages in his line have to furnish camels and horses; the Nazir requires twice as many, or five times as many, as are really wanted, and is bribed to reduce his demand. If the village is rich and bribes highly, it furnishes none, and the burden falls on those who cannot buy themselves off; they are forced to travel with their beasts for ten or for twenty days, unpaid, carrying their own food and that of their beasts, or plundering it, and are discharged perhaps 100 miles from home, their cattle and themselves lame and worn out. The amount of tyranny may be inferred from the depopulation. You see vast districts without an inhabitant, in which are the traces of a large and civilized people, great works for irrigation now in ruins, and constant remains of deserted towns. There is a city near the frontier with high walls and large stone houses, now absolutely uninhabited; it had once 60,000 inhabitants. There is not a palace on the Bosphorus that has not decimated the inhabitants of a province.'

A like spectacle is presented in the Troad. In the same volume from which the last extract has been taken, Mr Senior reports a conversation which he had with Mr Calvert in these words: *—' "The Turks are dying out, and the Greeks, many of them immigrants from European Turkey, are increasing. In your ride round the plain of Troy to-morrow, in a circuit of thirty miles you will find three Greek villages, Runkoi, Yenekoi, and Yenisher, all thriving, surrounded by gardens and cultivated fields, the old houses in repair and new ones building. The only other human habitations that you will see will be three Turkish villages—Chiflic, on the site of the Ilium Novum, Bounar Bashi, just below the site of Troy, and Halil Eli. The first has about twenty inhabited houses, the second about fifteen, and the third, which, twenty years ago, was a considerable village, has only three." '

Let us turn to another of the provinces of this empire. On leaving Constantinople Mr Senior reports the words of a friend well acquainted with the whole of Turkey :—' "You are going," he continued, "to Smyrna and to Greece. When you are at Smyrna, visit Ephesus. You will ride through fifty miles of the most fertile soil, blessed with the finest climate in the world. You will not see an inhabitant nor a cultivated field. This is Turkey.

* Senior, p. 163.

THE DECAY OF TURKEY. 49

In Greece, or in the Principalities, you will find comparative numbers, wealth, and population. They have been misgoverned; they have been the seat of war; but they have thrown off the Turk."'*

And again:—'In towns where there were 3000 Turks five or six years ago, there are now not 2000.†... In the provinces of the Dardanelles, the deaths exceed the births by about six per cent.

'When we recollect that the Greek population is increasing, and, therefore, that the Turks alone suffer this excess of deaths, we may infer that they are, as has often been said to me, rapidly dying out.' ‡

Nor is all this the inevitable result of any past policy which has now been abandoned. It exists still. The progress of ruin is going on before our eyes. Nay, it gathers force every day. Mr Skene contrasts the state of the country round Aleppo with what it was only twenty years before the date of his report. Within that district, he says, 'one hundred villages' had been entirely obliterated during the period of twenty years. The desolation is inseparable from Turkish rule in the nineteenth century. It is not the consequence of Mussulman power

* Senior, p. 148. † Ibid. p. 191. ‡ Ibid. p. 184.

merely, it is distinctively Turkish. During the brief rule of Mehemet Ali, Syria was beginning to be repeopled, and its waste places to be cultivated. Mr Brant, our consul at Damascus, writing in June, 1858, says:—'I have already sent a report on the trade of Damascus, but I conceive it would be incomplete were I not to add a sketch of the state and administration of the Paschalic. In the report I said that, while the province was in the occupation of Mehemet Ali Pasha, many deserted cities and villages were reinhabited, and their lands brought again under cultivation. This was particularly the case in the Haurân, in the country round Hamah, and generally on the confines of the Desert. In these places the Arabs were made to respect authority, and the settled inhabitants were effectually secured against their depredations.

'The whole of Syria was placed under the civil administration of Sheriff Pasha, and Ibrahim Pasha commanded the army, which amounted to 40,000 troops, regular and irregular. The able administration of the former increased the prosperity and improved the finances of the country as much as the activity and energy of the latter promoted security and confidence. The Government was certainly considered harsh, but it could scarcely, indeed, have been otherwise regarded, for it had to reform so many abuses, and to substitute system and equity for the disorder, license, and fanaticism which prevailed. The upper grades, the Effendis and Aghas, were most discontented, for they enriched themselves by the plunder and oppression of the industrious classes; but the latter were pleased to find themselves freed from the tyranny they had so long groaned under, and the Christians were particularly delighted at being shielded from the fanaticism which had reduced them to a state of intolerable degradation. The peasantry were not less contented; for, although the fixed taxes were rigorously exacted, no more was demanded, and no one was allowed to seize their produce without payment, to extort from them anything at less than its value, or to force them to render services without a fair remuneration. The Mussulmans were subjected to a conscription, then a novelty, which was a source of serious discontent, but the Christians paying Haratch were exempt from military service. The peasants who had reoccupied abandoned villages were assisted with loans to repair the houses and to supply themselves with stock, and enjoyed besides immunity from taxes for three years; every encouragement, in short, was held out to increase production, and sometimes even troops, with Ibrahim Pasha at their head, went out to destroy the eggs and young of the locusts.

'Under a system so vigorous, equitable, and considerate, the country was gradually advancing in prosperity, and, had the Egyptian rule continued, Syria would have regained a great portion of its ancient populousness and wealth, of which evident traces are visible in the remains of innumerable villages and cities spread over the Haurân, as well as to be found far to the eastward in the Desert, where also Roman roads are yet to be traced.' *

Then came the bombardment of Acre by the British fleet, the departure of the Egyptians, and the restoration of Syria to Turkish rule, with what effect the same witness reports :—' Scarcely were the Egyptians expelled and the strong arm removed, which had kept every one in due subordination to the ruling Power, than resistance to authority began to replace obedience, peculation and waste to be substituted for honesty and economy in the administration of the finances, revenue to decrease, the Arabs again to encroach on the settled inhabitants, the newly repeopled villages and lands to be gradually

* Despatches respecting apprehended disturbances in Syria, pp. 22, 23.

abandoned, until, at the present moment, there is so little security for person and property, that it may almost be said no longer to exist, and everything indicates a return to the state of anarchy in which the Egyptians found the country.'

* * * * * *

'The revenue is daily diminishing, from villages and lands being thrown out of cultivation. What is collected is in a great degree misapplied or plundered by the employés. Money is required from Constantinople to carry on the Government, and it is too evident that financial matters must progressively deteriorate, for the evils of a corrupt administration are constantly extending.' *

Whatever energy and self-reliance the Turks once possessed has long since gone. To use again the language of Mr Senior:—'Until the battle of Lepanto and the retreat from Vienna, they possessed the grand and heroic but dangerous virtues of a conquering nation. They are now degraded by the grovelling vices of a nation that relies on foreigners for its defence. But as respects the qualities which conduce to material prosperity, to riches and to numbers, I do not believe that they have much

* Despatches respecting apprehended disturbances in Syria, p. 23.

changed. I do not believe that they are more idle, wasteful, improvident, and brutal now than they were 400 years ago. But it is only within the last fifty years, that the effects of these qualities have shown themselves fully. When they first swarmed over Asia Minor, Roumelia, and Bulgaria, they seized on a country very populous and of enormous wealth. For 350 years they kept on consuming that wealth and wearing out that population. If a Turk wanted a house or a garden, he turned out a Rayah; if he wanted money, he put a bullet into a handkerchief, tied it into a knot, and sent it to the nearest opulent Greek or Armenian. At last, having lived for three centuries and a half on their capital of things and of man, having reduced that rich and well-peopled country to the desert which you now see it, they find themselves poor. They cannot dig, to beg they are ashamed. They use the most mischievous means to prevent large families; they kill their female children, the conscription takes off the males, and they disappear. The only memorial of what fifty years ago was a popular Turkish village is a crowded burial-ground, now unused.

' "As a medical man," said Y., "I, and perhaps *I* only, know what crimes are committed in the Turkish part of Smyrna, which looks so gay and smiling, as its picturesque houses, embosomed in gardens of planes and cypresses, rise up the hill. I avoid as much as I can the Turkish houses, that I may not be cognisant of them. Sometimes it is a young second wife who is poisoned by the older one; sometimes a female child, whom the father will not bring up; sometimes a male killed by the mother to spite the father. Infanticide is rather the rule than the exception. No inquiry is made, no notice is taken by the police." ' *

But it is impossible to give all the facts which may be gathered from the Parliamentary papers issued of late years on the state of Syria and of Turkey in general, and to cite the evidence of witnesses worthy of confidence. Nor, indeed, is it necessary to accumulate evidence on a point about which there is no dispute. To use the words of the late Lord Carlisle when surveying, not a province merely, but the whole extent of the Turkish empire:—' When you leave the partial splendours of the capital, and the great state establishments, what is it you find over this broad surface of a land, which nature and climate have favoured beyond all others, once the home of all art and all civilization? Look yourself—ask those who live there;—deserted vil-

* Senior, pp. 211-12.

lages, uncultivated plains, banditti-haunted mountains, torpid laws, a corrupt administration, a disappearing people.'*

This, then, is the testimony which even the physical features of the country bear against the Turkish rule. In the nineteenth century, large tracts of what, thirty, twenty—nay, ten—years ago was a smiling and a fruitful land, cultivated with all the care of garden husbandry, and rivalling for beauty the best parts of the plains of Lombardy and of Flanders, have now become portions of the desert. From the shores of the Bosphorus, under the fairest sky, amid the most beautiful scenery, with a soil the most fertile of any in the world, surrounded by the ruins of ancient glory and civilization, the traveller now may wander for more than a hundred miles without meeting with a trace of the dwellings of man, save here and there the ruins which his horse tramples under its hoofs. If he asks for the inhabitants, he will hear only of graves, of heartless massacres, and of terrible martyrdoms on a gigantic scale, with pashas for the executioners, and grand viziers for the instigators. The desert is rapidly encroaching on the fertile land, and the sand is

* Diary in Turkish and Greek Waters, by the Earl of Carlisle. Second edition. London, 1854. P. 184.

THE DECAY OF TURKEY. 57

covering what was, a quarter of a century ago, the abode of industrious and happy peasants. The land was 'as the garden of Eden;' it is now 'a desolate wilderness.'

In 1830 Smyrna contained 80,000 Turkish inhabitants and 20,000 Christians. In 1860 the Turks numbered 41,000 and the Christians 75,000.* Though the Christians have increased at this enormous rate within thirty years, this increase has been almost neutralized by the great decline of the Turkish part of the inhabitants in the same period of time; and the decline is even greater in the smaller towns and villages than in Smyrna. The same consul from whose report these statistics are taken, remarks :—' It may be observed, in reference to this question, that rapid as the increase is of the Christian population, the decrease of the Turkish is in a greater ratio. Visit any town or village where there is a mixed Mussulman and Christian population: in the Turkish quarter no one is visible, no children in the streets; whereas in the Christian the streets are full of children.'†

This is not peculiar to Smyrna or to the country

* Report of Mr Charles Blunt, Consul at Smyrna. Parliamentary Papers on Condition of Christians in Turkey, p. 31.
† Ibid. p. 32.

in its neighbourhood. This decline of the one race and the increase of the other is uniform throughout Turkey:—'On the continent, in the islands, it is the Greek peasant who works and thrives; the Turk reclines, smokes his pipe, and decays. The Greek village increases its population, and teems with children; in the Turkish village you find roofless walls and crumbling mosques.'*

'As we rode through one of the villages from which the Turkish inhabitants have disappeared, my companion chimed in with the universal view of the rapid decay of their numbers. He gives them from twenty-five to forty years before, without the help of war or violence, they would entirely vanish from the land.' †

This opinion is supported by the testimony of Mr Finn, who, speaking of the province of Palestine, tells us that there also—'The Mahometan population is dying out; I can scarcely say slowly.' ‡

To the same effect, again, Mr J. E. Blunt, writing from Pristina, says:—'While everywhere

* Lord Carlisle, Diary in Turkish and Greek Waters, p. 183.
† Ibid. p. 171.
‡ Despatches on apprehended disturbances in Syria, 1858 to 1860, p. 89.

there are signs that the Turks, more especially the higher classes, are losing ground in population, agriculture, and trade, the opposite is the case with the Christians.

'In nearly all the towns, streets—entire quarters —have passed into the hands of the Christians.'*

The language of Sir George Bowen, the present Governor of Queensland, written a few years ago, will form a fitting conclusion to this chapter. He says, 'We trust that the time is not very remote, when civilization, advancing gradually eastward, will achieve a bloodless conquest in those European provinces, where the finest country in the world has long, under the barbarous despotism of the Turk, been more wasted by peace than other lands have been wasted by war; where science is unknown; where arts and manufactures languish; where agriculture decays; where the human race itself melts away.'†

* Consular Reports on Condition of Christians of Turkey, p. 36.
† Mount Athos, Thessaly, and Epirus, p. 245.

CHAPTER III.

DECLINE OF THE TURKISH RACE.

NOTWITHSTANDING the increase of the Christian subjects of Turkey, which but for the destruction of life by massacres and wholesale murder would be far larger, the population throughout the empire is still diminishing, and that in consequence of the enormous decrease of the Mussulmans. Thus this depopulation arises from two different causes:—(1) From the dying out of the dominant race; and this diminution of the number of the Turkish inhabitants is going on at so rapid a rate as to threaten their total extinction within a comparatively short time. (2) From the frequent massacres of Christians, either such as are heard of in Europe because of the large number of lives which are lost—like those which took place some eighteen years ago in the Lebanon, in Damascus, at Jeddah, and other places in Asia, and that in Bulgaria during the spring of the present year—or those massacres which occur daily on a smaller scale, but which in the aggregate are even more destructive to life than those which led to the French occupation of Syria, and furnished much anxious employment to diplomatists. Of these two elements of ruin, it will be necessary to speak only of the first, which, from its nature, is generally kept out of sight in the account which travellers give us of that country. Most travellers and writers on Turkey act as Lord Carlisle did, who says, 'Upon the state of morals I debar myself from entering.'* And yet this is the most important matter for consideration when the state and prospects of an empire are to be examined. It is not surprising, however, that men who know what the state of morals is shrink from so repulsive a subject. I cannot pass it by; it would be unfair to do so. In it consists much of the misery which the Christians suffer. I cannot, however—I will not attempt to—give in detail that which it is in my power to give, mindful of the injunction, 'Uncleanness or covetousness ($\pi\lambda\epsilon o\nu\epsilon\xi\acute{\iota}a$), let it not be once named among you,

* Lord Carlisle, Diary in Turkish and Greek Waters, p. 182.

as becometh saints.'* I must content myself with vague words; the subject permits of no other.

Polygamy is said to be generally less conducive to the increase of mankind than monogamy. The wide-spread practice of infanticide amongst all classes is a reason why the Turkish part of the population should not merely be stationary but diminish. Conscription for the army, which is raised entirely from the Mussulman portion of the population, has also an important influence in the same direction. But all these causes combined will not account for the fact that the Turks are rapidly becoming extinct. At best, these causes would but check or diminish the natural rate of increase. The evil lies far deeper. It is one, however, which cannot be laid bare. The hideous revolting profligacy of all classes, and almost every individual in every class, is the main cause for the diminution. This is a canker which has eaten into the very vitals of society. It is one, however, which has taken so loathsome a form that no pen dares describe the immoral state of Turkish society. It must be abandoned to vague generalities, for happily the imagination cannot picture the abominations which are fast exterminating the whole Turk-

* Ephes. v. 3.

ish race. If, at the certainty of outraging decency, some hints even were given, they would necessarily fall so far short of the truth that they would have the effect of eulogy by making men believe that the horrid details of guilt revealed in any degree the real corruption of this deeply polluted race. I speak thus advisedly.

I have the evidence now before me of persons at present resident in Turkey, as well as of English officers high in the civil service, whose duties have made them acquainted with the real state of society in Turkey; and in addition to these, I have a voluminous report addressed to me by a distinguished foreigner, formerly a colonel in the Turkish service, and, from the varied offices which he has filled in that country, of all men one of the most competent witnesses. I have all this evidence before me, but it is so disgusting and obscene that I dare not make use of it. The Satires of Juvenal and Petronius Arbiter are decorous in comparison. Students may remember how rabbinical writers describe the sins of the Amorites and other inhabitants of the land of Canaan, who for their revolting sins were driven out by the children of Israel.* That description gives

* As, for instance, Maimonides, in 'More Nevochim,' § Precepts of the second class.

but a partial picture of what is the present state of Turkish society. The Cities of the Plain were destroyed for sins which are the common, normal, every-day practice of this people.

And, be it remembered, I am not speaking of the dregs of society—the outcasts of humanity—herding together at Constantinople or Damascus; I speak of grand viziers, of powerful pashas, of many of the present ministers of the Sultan. I read often in Blue Books and in the speeches of the supporters of Turkey, of —— Pasha, the friend of England; or —— Pasha, the enlightened Minister for —— Affairs. I am told of their intelligence, but no one will become sponsor for their honesty, still less for their morality. The utmost that could be said by an English Ambassador, whose words have been already quoted, was, that what they '*ostentatiously and constantly*' assert can hardly be untrue. This is the first time, so far as my experience serves, that ostentatiousness has been supposed to be a guarantee for the truthfulness of any statement. But it is not necessary to call the English Ambassador as a witness in this matter. It is perfectly notorious that these pashas, these ministers, are men so foul and obscene in their lives, that the 'most infamous

DECLINE OF THE TURKISH RACE. 65

ruffians of the Haymarket'* would shrink from them as beings sunk immeasurably beneath themselves, and as too polluted for companionship. And yet these advisers of the Sultan are the men who were eulogized by Mr Layard in the House of Commons as 'good and worthy.'† That gentleman's standard of goodness and of worth seems a peculiar one. Several at least of the present advisers of the Sultan were educated in the harem (the rest of my sentence must of necessity be in a dead language) atque ibi cinædi et pathici juventutem agebant. Iisdem in gubernationem regni promovendis primus ad honores et imperia gradus extitit quod libidini regiæ morigerentur. Ea autem ipsa flagitia quibus in pueritiâ et adolescentiâ sunt imbuti maturi viri consequuntur, et pueros haud paucos, in quibus libidinem exerceant, æquè ac puellas, in domûs secretiore parte conservare solent.‡ If these are the 'good and worthy men' of Turkey, what are the ordinary inhabitants of that country? And what

* See Mr Gregory's Speech in the House of Commons, May 29, 1863.
† See Mr Layard's Speech, in *Morning Star*, May 30, 1863.
‡ These words were applied to the Ministers of the Porte of 1862. I have no knowledge as to the present Ministers.

5

honesty, what forbearance, what truth can be expected when these are the rulers of the Ottoman Empire? But I dare not pursue this subject.

In a letter already quoted, which was read by Mr Cobden in the House of Commons on the occasion of a debate on the Eastern Question, occurs the following passage:—'Few of you in England know the real horrors of this country. You will see what I mean when I tell you my intention of getting a number of tracts, in Turkish, written or lithographed, to be distributed by a Turk on the bridges, &c. The tract is to consist of such passages as the history of Sodom and Gomorrah. What can we hope to do with this people? One Englishman, who has to do with multitudes of them, reckons those who are innocent of this hideous vice at two in a hundred. A Turkish teacher told an European that those who were guiltless as to that are two in a thousand. Stories of assaults, *sub dio*, effected or attempted, have come to me one after another. These people must be held together? What is our policy supporting? Are we not responsible for corruption which breeds by our fostering? Some one asked me how to account for this in a people the most moral of all—the English people—that these deepest immoralities should be maintained by their patronage? I replied, they are for the most part quite ignorant, or unwilling to believe what they hear. Still, it is a condition of morals which makes khans and baths and lonely places dangerous to the unwary. . . .

' . . . Believe me (my authority is the best), it is a question of time; the decay of the Turkish people is going on rapidly; their numbers are fast decreasing through vice, disease, neglect, and the conscription.' *

It is painful to print even this extract, though what it reveals is only an approximation to the horrors and licentiousness of Turkish society. It is better, however, to shock the reader rather than that, through ignorance, we should continue to 'maintain,' to 'foster,' and to 'patronize' such a condition of society. Half the world knows what we are doing: it is high time that we were also conscious, and that we should consider whether any theory, or fancy, or chimera about the balance of power, or the 'integrity of Turkey,' will justify our maintenance of such unspeakable wickedness.

It is this corruption, this revolting form of brutal sensuality, which makes the presence of a Turkish

* Letter addressed to Rev. Ernest Hawkins, 8th January, 1863, MSS. in Archives of the Society for the Propagation of the Gospel.

garrison so grievous a wrong to the Christians in its neighbourhood. If in Constantinople—in the chief city of the empire—in the presence of European civilization, a state of things exists which 'makes khans and baths and lonely places dangerous to the unwary,' what must be the condition of the people who, in Servia, in Bulgaria, or in Syria, live near these abodes of sin and pollution, with a fierce fanatical soldiery free from all moral restraints, and encouraged by their officers in every act of hostility towards the Christians? It is unnatural horrors of this kind, even more than the numerous murders and acts of rapine which mark the presence of a Turkish garrison, against which the inhabitants of Belgrade and the Prince of Servia protested. They prayed, until at length the Turkish garrison was withdrawn from that city, that their young children might be spared the sight of deeds which defiled at times the esplanade of the fortress. They prayed that they might have some safeguard that their sons may no longer be carried off. . . .

It cannot be that the other races who inhabit Turkey will always pray in vain to a Christian people. If treaties be pleaded as a hindrance to our active assistance in their behalf, let us at any rate not encourage the wrongdoers in the perpetration of these acts of abomination and wickedness. Nay, rather let the sight and the love which we bear our own children, sheltered happily from such dangers, quicken our sympathies for the oppressed, and move us to desire at least that they may soon possess that liberty which is our inheritance; but, above all, that they may obtain that freedom from the contamination of those horrid forms of vice to which all are exposed who are forced to live in contact with Turks.

So far as can be gathered from the testimony of travellers, from the evidence furnished by Parliamentary papers, and from the imperfect statistics which we possess of various provinces of Turkey, as well as from the refusal to allow any statistical returns to be officially made, lest they should reveal the real condition of the empire, the Turkish element in the population will be extinct within sixty years; and should the present rate of decrease continue, within less than one generation the Ottoman power will necessarily have ceased to exist. The question, a deeply interesting one to ourselves, naturally suggests itself—What is to be the policy of England under these circumstances? Is another generation of Turkish subjects to be reared under their present oppressors, and the whole nation be educated in bitter hostility and hatred to England because of the support, I will not call it moral, which we give to this loathsome despotism.

Let us remember—'At no distant time the Greeks will govern this country. What we have to wish is that they should come to the government with English feelings, English opinions, and English sympathies. The Russians through their political agents, the French through their missionaries and schools, are striving to make them hate and despise us.'*

Judging from the policy of our public men we seem desirous of teaching the future masters of Asia Minor, of Syria, and of Roumelia to 'hate and despise us.' An impression prevails throughout Turkey that England is the firm and unscrupulous ally of the Sultan. Young Turkey—the scoffing Mussulman who has broken away from even the restraint of the Koran—with a significant gesture indicative of the most polluted idea, passes his judgment upon the unnatural alliance of England and Turkey, and pays us the compliment of exclaiming, 'We are all brothers, the English and the Tosques—we are all Framasouns (infidels).' † When the Druse chieftains

* Senior, p. 219.
† Layard's Nineveh. Vol. I. p. 163. Third edition.

massacred, with unspeakable atrocities, the Christians of the Lebanon, it was done not only at the instigation of the Court of Constantinople, but with the belief that it would be pleasing to the Queen of England, who, as the ruler of that 'infidel' nation, and the devoted ally, and, as they believe, tributary of the Sultan, must needs rejoice at the slaughter of the Christians.* After the massacres in Bulgaria the Turkish newspapers published an alleged telegram from Windsor to the effect that, come what might, the Queen of England had promised not to desert the cause of the Sultan, and the Bashi-bazouks, according to the correspondent of the *Times* at Constantinople, went to the war against Servia with the conviction that England had even guaranteed them their pay. If this is the belief, the firm belief, of the ruling race—and if, unhappily, our actions as a nation give currency to this notion—it is not to be wondered if the subject race should be reared in the same belief, and that they should begin to look upon the people of this country as their natural and implacable foes; the more hateful because gratuitously joining in acts of wrong from which no benefit can accrue; for, of all persecutors, the amateur persecutor

* Correspondence on the Affairs of Syria, June, 1860, p. 55.

is the most intolerable. There are sad indications that this belief is gaining ground. Let me first speak of my own experience. A few years ago I visited three of the Servian monasteries, having received from the Metropolitan of Servia a letter of commendation to all the clergy of that country. 'On my presenting the letter of the archbishop to a monk at one of these monasteries (Rakowitza), he remarked that he had read much about the English nation, but had never before met with any of my fellow-countrymen, as few Englishmen ever came to Servia. "And what has led you," said he, "to this country?" I answered, that I had come partly in quest of health, and partly to see something more of the state of the Greek Church. "Then am I to understand," he rejoined, "that, though an Englishman, you are a friend of Servia?" I told him that I knew no reason why an Englishman should be held to be hostile to Servia. "How, then," he added, "is it I find in the newspapers that whenever any act of oppression and cruelty by the Turks towards our people is complained of, members of the British Parliament always rise up to excuse and justify the Turks? Why is it," he continued, with animation, "you who are the great, the greatest civilizers in Europe, invariably support the cause of those who are most hostile to all civilization—the Turks—against us, who are doing our best to follow your example?"'*

This is a wide-spread feeling amongst all classes. I cite, from the letter of a friend, a recent instance of the same feeling in Asia:—'On one occasion lately, an English traveller arrived at the house of an American missionary. He was hospitably welcomed, but before he had been long in the house where he intended to sleep he observed that there was a domestic commotion, and anxiety on the face of the missionary. It was evident that, in some way or another, he was the cause of this. He therefore insisted on an explanation, when the latter informed him that the servants had mutinied—they refused to do anything for one of the *enemies of Christianity*, an Englishman. Such is the result of our Eastern policy.'

Instances of this kind might be multiplied without end. Fortunately, this hostility, which our recent policy is engendering, is only in the bud. The Christians of the East, from Montenegro to the borders of Persia, still turn their eyes to England in all their sufferings; and proportionably to their ex-

* Servia and the Servians. By the Rev. W. Denton, p. 237.

pectations, their feelings are made bitter by disappointment. To them, France is known chiefly as the advocate of the Roman Church and the armed assertor of Papal supremacy, and this will always interpose a barrier between that nation and the Christians of the East. Russia they dread as a gigantic power on their frontier, which would absorb them, to the loss of all national existence, and they turn away from her with fear, proportionate to her nearness and her strength. Austria, chiefly known to the people on the borders of the Danube by petty, stupid, vexatious acts of tyranny, as well as by her religious intolerance, is more odious than Russia, though in her case hatred is softened down and mitigated by contempt. England, from its distance, from the nature of its Government, and its separation from Rome, as well as because of its material interests in the trade of these nations, is regarded as their natural protector. This is a feeling to be fostered, not to be turned awry and embittered, to serve the interests of a few individuals amongst ourselves, or to satisfy the unreasoning prejudices of the many.

But if the indifference to the condition of the Christians of Turkey is so general in this country, and if the belief in the necessity of maintaining what is called ' the integrity of Turkey ' is so deeply rooted in the minds of Englishmen, how, it may be asked, has this arisen? How comes it that this opinion has so much vitality? It springs from one cause: the people of this country are taught to believe that the Christians of Turkey are conspirators against what Sir Henry Bulwer calls the 'tolerant' rule of the Sultan for the purpose of aggrandizing Russia. This one assertion, iterated by interested speculators and repeated by unreasoning politicians, deafen the ears of Englishmen to the testimony of unprejudiced travellers, blinds their eyes to notorious facts, and dulls their intellect to the voice of reason. The supporters of Turkey know the value of this 'idol of the imagination,' and are always ready to brandish it before our eyes whenever we appear disposed to act independently, and in the interests of humanity, which is one with that of England. When it was desirable that 'our consular agents' should testify that Turkish rule was 'tolerant,' that the Christians were not oppressed, and that the assertions of the Russian note were untrue, this fear was skilfully played upon. In the circular of the 11th of June, addressed to 'our consular agents,' the Ambassador informs them in words which, if true, must have sounded to them superfluous:—'I have also been made acquainted, through the channel of our consular agents, as well as by other means, that great efforts have of late been made by persons of various kinds—not identified with, or belonging to, the native population—to get up discontent amongst the population, and to excite them to make complaints that may reach the ear of the European Powers; and that in this way the Slave population has been especially brought to imagine that it may obtain, through foreign protection, great advantages, and even arrive at an independent existence.

'I have likewise been informed that a conspiracy among the Slavonian race, with the object of making a revolution in this empire, actually exists—with chiefs selected, and plans more or less defined—and that though such conspiracy may not, at this moment, be formidable, its leaders imagine it may become so by exciting the sympathies of the great western and northern states.'

Let us, however, listen to the words of competent witnesses, recorded by Mr Senior. Speaking of the Christians in European Turkey, he says:—'They all, without any exception, hate Russia, and look for support and protection to England.*

'The Bulgarians hate not only the Russians, but the Greeks, and so do the Roumelians, until you

* Senior, p. 34.

reach Thessaly, where the Greek race prevails, and a desire for union with their brethren in the war of independence is naturally felt.

'"What is the feeling," I asked, "of Servia, Bosnia, and the Principalities?"

'"A general hatred of all their neighbours. They hate the Russians, the Austrians, the Greeks, and the Turks. What they really wish for is independence, at least the virtual independence which has been gained by Servia."'*

In the same volume Mr Whittall, of Smyrna, is cited as a witness to the same effect:—'The Greeks dream of nothing but a Greek empire, to be created by the help of Russia. They despise the Russians as slaves and savages, but they hope to make use of them, and then to throw them off.' †

The words of another person are quoted by Mr Senior to the same purpose:—'We sympathize with the Russians only as the enemies of the Turks. Their whole system of government, of trade, of thought, and of feeling is repulsive to us. Our strongest feeling is the desire to preserve our nationality; we have clung to it for 3000 years. If we are attached to the peculiarities of our religion, it is not because we care about the Patriarch of

* Senior, p. 35. † Ibid. p. 205.

Constantinople or about the doctrines which separate us from the Roman Catholics or from the Protestants, but because we think that those peculiarities are safeguards of our nationality. We shall not suffer ourselves to be merged in the semi-barbarous mass of Russia, or even to become one of its satellites.' *

And this is borne out by notorious facts. The provinces of Turkey are in a chronic state of discontent through the daily outrages perpetrated on the Christians, which are less the result of the fanaticism of the Mussulman people than of the deliberate policy of the Sultan and his Ministers. At no period during the present century was there more quiet in these provinces than during the war in the Crimea, when the Turkish troops occupied in struggling against the Russians were withdrawn from the interior of Turkey. Now, had there existed any understanding with Russia, surely Bulgaria, Servia, Bosnia, Epirus, and Syria would have risen in arms; and, by so doing, have seriously embarrassed the Western Powers. They remained quiet, however. It was no part of their policy to unite with Russia, and this alone kept these provinces from revolt, although denuded of Turkish

* Senior, p. 215.

troops.* The Montenegrins, it is notorious, have refused all offers of Russian protection, with the proud declaration that they would remain independent both of Turkey and of Russia. A few years ago we were all of us taught to believe that Greece was but the vassal and bond-slave of Russia, and that all intrigues in that country were but to pave the way for some imaginary prince from St Petersburg or Moscow, who should convert Greece, from being 'a mere outpost of Russia,' into an integral part of that empire. I hope we are all of us ashamed of our old belief. I trust we shall for the future show less credulous confidence in our blind guides. This notion is getting too absurd to be maintained any longer. It is hardly worthy of serious refutation. Men may in desperation rush from grievous tyranny to some milder form of despotism, because unable to achieve their entire freedom; but races half emancipated, provinces virtually independent, are not prone to immolate themselves, and to quench their young life, by voluntary submission to a new

* 'In the Crimean War the Servians resisted every attempt to induce them to arm against the Turks in favour of Russia... They steadily refused to take part in any war against Turkey, and remained faithful throughout the war to the Suzerain power.'—*Speech of A. H. Layard, Esq.* Murray, 1863.

master. History gives us no instances of such madness, and we can but appeal to experience on such a matter. Let us therefore dismiss this delusion to the limbo of ghosts, as a bugbear which may be useful to terrify children, but which ought to be powerless to make men turn aside from the path of right; for in fact, the notion that Servia, that Bulgaria, Bosnia, or Asia Minor, have secret relations with Russia, is so evidently a delusion, that it does not allow of serious argument. We have lived to see table-turning practised and spirit-rapping believed in, but to contend that there is a spirit-medium between Russia and the Christians of the East, is to own that we have sunk even below the credulity of those who think that mahogany and oak are in conspiracy with angels or demons, and that articles of domestic furniture really turn round through the effect of 'foreign intrigues.'

In truth, neither the agents of Russia nor of any other Power could persuade the large Christian communities in Turkey to be dissatisfied with their lot, unless there existed causes for discontent. The fact that these races, widely separated from each other and possessing few means of intercourse, are all of them profoundly dissatisfied with their lot, is, at least, some ground for believing that their condition is one

DECLINE OF THE TURKISH RACE. 81

of suffering and of injustice. Nations goaded to madness by oppression are often mistaken in the remedies to which they resort for deliverance from their wrongs; but no intrigues can persuade a nation that justice is injustice—that right is wrong—and that freedom is bondage.

Here, however, we are not left to the testimony of the sufferers themselves. The pains and penalties attaching to the profession of Christianity are too patent: the sharp cry of anguish has so often reached even the ears of the people of Western Europe, that we cannot refuse to believe in the existence of wide-spread, capricious, and bitter suffering. Hence for the last thirty years the public feeling of Europe has constantly demanded an amelioration of the hard lot of the Christian subjects of the Porte. The assistance rendered to Turkey by this country at the time of the Crimean war was fettered with this one condition, that as a return for such assistance the Government of that country should guarantee, I will not say equality, but a removal of some of the more galling inequalities of the position of the people of Turkey. This has been promised by the Ministers of successive Sultans, this has been embodied in solemn public treaties with the Great Powers of

Christendom, this has been written in Hatt-i-Sherifs, Hatt-i-Humaïouns, and—not one item of these treaties, not one single provision of any of these Hatts, have ever been fulfilled by the Government of Turkey.

CHAPTER IV.

FOREIGN INTRIGUES.

It is an ever-ready but a vulgar excuse to attribute all popular discontent to 'foreign intrigues.' That foreign agents may stimulate the urgency of an oppressed people for redress is possible, but their power is limited; they can do no more than this, and these foreign agents will be disarmed when people cease to suffer. In place, then, of attributing the notorious dissatisfaction, the wide-spread discontent, of the Christians of Turkey to 'foreign intrigues,' it would be more to the purpose to inquire whether there does not exist ample and legitimate grounds for such dissatisfaction.

When in England we hear of brigandage in Bosnia, of sullen discontent in Bulgaria, we are told it is the work of Russian agents and of Muscovite intrigues. Russia probably denies the charge and retorts the accusation, pointing in support of her belief that England is intriguing in Turkey, to the notorious partiality of the Foreign Office of this country, the readiness with which every abominable and atrocious act of the governors of Turkey is palliated, and actions the simplest and most natural of an oppressed people are exaggerated by British officials. France certainly makes the same charges against England which English politicians make against Russia, and is as uneasy at the success of English intrigue as any minister of state in this country can be at the progress of Russian agents.* All this may possibly arise from the jealousy with which men watch the actions of a rival, and satisfy themselves by attributing evil motives where they are unable to point to evil actions. On this subject let us listen, I will not say even to the testimony of men of intelligence,

* 'What is the complaint? In 1840 there was a Turkey and a Turkish Government, in 1862 there remains nothing but England and an English Government. The East can on longer face decrepit mouldering Turkey, but it has to encounter vigorous and powerful England. Greece, Egypt, Syria, the Lebanon, Servia, the Danubian provinces, no longer look to Constantinople, but to London. Turkey has found the secret of being even more formidable than she was in the 18th or 16th century, by being nothing of herself, and of being everything through England.'—ST MARC GIRARDIN, *Revue des Deux Mondes*, Oct. 1862.

but to the voice of common sense, for, in truth, this childish accusation of 'foreign intrigue' is not only beside the purpose, as wholly insufficient to account for the discontent which reigns throughout Turkey, but it is one which it is so easy to make, so difficult to substantiate, so impossible to disprove, that it cannot be allowed to stand, as it now does, instead of facts, in the place of information, and as a substitute for reason. The suggestion of such 'intrigues' is often made by English consuls and other agents in defiance of evidence to the contrary. Compare for a moment the confession of Turkish ministers as to the cause of the outbreak in the Herzegovina which led to the present war between Servia and the Porte with the suggestion of Mr Holmes, the English consul at Bosna Serai. Whereas the first Secretary of the Sultan, writing to the Grand Vizier, declares 'that the causes which produce trouble among *the peaceful population* are in a great measure due to the unseemly conduct of some incapable functionaries, and particularly to the exactions to which the avaricious farmers of taxes lend themselves in the hope of a larger profit.'*
Mr Holmes is sure it is all the work of 'Servian agitators.' †

* Correspondence respecting affairs in Bosnia and Herzegovina, 1876, p. 17.
† Ibid. p. 23.

I am reminded by these words of Mr Holmes of a pleasant anecdote which I was told by the person chiefly concerned, at least the only one concerned who is now alive. Some few years ago a young *attaché* of a foreign embassy to this country, now one of the foremost diplomatists in Europe, was going by rail to Southampton. It chanced that at the same time several of her Majesty's ministers were on their way to Osborne. Lord Palmerston had in his jaunty manner referred a few nights before in the House of Commons to 'Russian intrigues.' On this the young and zealous diplomatist proceeded to lecture his Lordship, since, as he alleged, the fact was notoriously in opposition to this statement. 'I know—I know,' replied the Prime Minister, 'but one can do anything one likes with the Commons if only you tell them of Russian intrigues.' Lord Palmerston was probably joking at the young *attaché's* expense, but the jest was a truth notwithstanding. It settles everything. It atones for our shortcomings, it excuses our injustice, it saves us the trouble of thinking, it invests our unwisdom with the appearance of policy, if only we whisper, 'Russian intrigues.'

The question then, I repeat, is not whether the Christians of Turkey are ever inflamed against the

Government of the Sultan by 'foreign intrigues,' but whether, without any such 'intrigues,' there exist grounds for such discontent; whether every province of Turkey, from the banks of the Danube to the Red Sea, is not suffering from the gross injustice of the Government towards the people; whether the Christians of Turkey are not oppressed by such rapacious rulers, that men would cease to be men if they were not discontented, and that whether, under such a condition of existence, 'foreign intrigues' would not be needless, a mere work of supererogation.

Now what do we find revealed to us in the report of our own consuls, and in the recently-published books of men of sagacity and integrity? Not only the evidence of wide-spread dissatisfaction and discontent, but ample grounds for this feeling. The people of Turkey are discontented because they know that certain rights—the simplest rights which humanity can claim—have been promised, and are withheld from them by the Government of the Sultan. So long as this grievance remains, it will require no 'foreign intrigues' to make them dissatisfied. For though the Hatt-i-humaïoun has not been even read, 'it cannot be a dead letter . . . it stimulates the hopes, and also the hatred, of the

Greeks. They see that the Turks are resolved to render illusory stipulations made by the Allies in their favour. They are,' consequently, 'if possible, worse subjects of the Sultan than they were before the war.'*

The Christians of Turkey, again, are naturally discontented, because they know that the Government of Turkey is utterly indifferent to their cries for redress; that no official throughout that country troubles himself to ascertain how many of them are murdered, still less to punish any one for the murder of a Christian unless some active and troublesome consul interfere. Except in this case, which is necessarily of rare occurrence, the life of a Christian may be taken with perfect impunity. In one district, Mr Rogers reports that eleven hundred of such murders have taken place within nineteen years, 'not one of which has been avenged by law.'†
Of another district, a most competent witness, Dr Dickson, of Smyrna, reporting the murder of a Greek woman under circumstances of great atrocity and the discovery of the murderer, says, 'He will be released; no Mussulman cares about the murder of a

---

* Senior, p. 152.

† Correspondence on Affairs of Syria, 1860, 1861, p. 404.

Rayah.'* At Beyrout the British consul reports nine murders, and remarks, 'Unfortunately, no effective steps are taken by the Turkish authorities to repress these disorders by the capture and infliction of condign punishment on delinquents; indeed, Mr Abela, the vice-consul, states that the authorities in Sidon have become so accustomed to the commission of these atrocities, that they no longer seem to attach any gravity to them.'† There is no remedy for these wrongs whilst the present inequality between Mussulman and non-Mussulman subjects of the Porte is maintained. So long as Christian evidence is not received in a criminal court, there is the most perfect impunity for the murder of Christians.

It would be a mistake, however, for us to suppose for a moment that the relatives, the friends, and the co-religionists of the murdered persons are perfectly satisfied with this state of things, and are only made discontented, as English consuls and party politicians tell us, by reason of 'foreign intrigues.'

There is indeed widespread discontent, and,

* Senior, p. 68.
† Despatches on apprehended disturbances in Syria, 1858—1860, p. 95.

alas! ample cause for it. The facts we have on the testimony of the English consuls in Turkey.

Mr Holmes, writing from Bosna Serai, the capital of Bosnia, says:—'I have the honour to report to your Lordship that I find the position of affairs in this province to be most unsatisfactory, the opinion being generally prevalent that, without some powerful intervention, Bosnia and Herzegovina may soon witness scenes similar to those which have lately horrified Europe in Syria.

'Reports are continually arriving here of massacres of Christians in different places, which, if untrue, serve at least to show the existing excitement and alarm.

'On the night of the 6th the Ferik Pasha commanding the troops here left this suddenly by post, taking with him his son and a few attendants. The Vali Pasha declared that he had merely proceeded to the Servian frontier to inspect the troops and defensible positions in that direction, as several inroads had lately been made by bodies of Servian volunteers. This service, however, did not seem to call for a sudden and, as it were, secret departure at midnight, and the explanation of the Pasha was looked upon as an evasion of the truth. The next day a rumour was spread abroad that some twenty

Christians had been massacred at Gradiska, in the district of Banialuka, by the Turkish population. This excited great alarm here. The authorities were said to have denied the truth of the report, but its coincidence with the departure of the Ferik threw suspicion on their sincerity.'*

And again, a few weeks later, the same consul tells us:—' A few days after my arrival here I wrote a despatch dated the 18th August regarding the state of affairs in this Pashalic, from which you will have perceived that a good deal of alarm and excitement prevails. Since that date I have had further opportunities of observation. There is here, at present, no deliberate intention, though the desire may perhaps exist, on the part of the Mussulman population, to assault the lives or property of the Christian population; and I believe also that the chief danger lies in the agitated state of the public mind, of which, unfortunately, there is no doubt, and in connection with which the smallest accident may, at any moment, produce the most serious results. In addition to real causes of complaint every little accident is magnified into a premeditated crime; and dismal stories, no doubt often invented

* Report of Consuls on Condition of Christians in Turkey, pp. 47, 48.

and industriously circulated, are not wanting to increase the existing alarm.' *

Of the state of affairs in the same province, Mr Zohrab reports :—

* * * * * *

'The influence of the Central Government is daily becoming weaker, while the pride and fanaticism of the Bosniac Mussulmans is rapidly developing itself. Such a disregard to its interests will eventually bring against the Porte two formidable antagonists—the Christians, who have given up all hope of amelioration of their position under the present *régime*, and who are daily subjected to fresh hardships, and the Mussulmans, who look upon the Government of the Sultan with disdain. The presence of an energetic and honest Governor is urgently required in Bosnia. Such a man could render valuable service in re-establishing order, and in removing many of the causes of irritation; but if the Porte persists in sending Pashas, without regard to their capabilities, disgrace and misfortune must necessarily follow.' †

Of the country round Aleppo, Mr Skene writes: —' In the towns, until quite lately, trade and manu-

* Report of Consuls on Condition of Christians in Turkey, p. 69.   † Ibid. p. 70.

factures were in a flourishing state. Since the revival, however, of the old feelings of aversion and animosity between the Mussulman and Christian communities, a disadvantageous change has consequently become apparent also in the material circumstances of the population. Want of confidence in the future is withdrawing capital from circulation; trade stagnates; and one-half of the looms previously worked are now at rest.'*

Whilst murder, in every part of the Turkish empire, is unpunished; whilst crimes of every description are done with impunity on the persons of Christians; whilst they are liable to be thrust from their little property at any moment, and to be despoiled of the goods which they have collected; and whilst all the time the Government is under express treaty obligation to protect its subjects, and yet exerts no influence in this direction, we cannot wonder that the rule of the Sultan is everywhere despised:—'Mr Vice-Consul Rogers reports that throughout his recent journeys over unfrequented parts of the country he heard everywhere the desponding expressions of the peasantry, that—"There is no Government."—"Where is the

* Report of Consuls on Condition of Christians in Turkey, p. 49.

Government?"—"The Government is sunk into nothing,"—and this is confirmed by the facts of robberies on the roads, and the hostile combats of villages.' *

In the same strain Mr Finn, of Jerusalem, tells us:—'Respect for the Ottoman Government is gone; the plains are overrun by Bedaween, and these venture, as they never did before, to come in among villages and between the hills; those from beyond Jordan have even plundered cattle in large numbers within sight of the sea-port Jaffa.' †

In another direction we have testimony to the same effect. Mr Calvert, of Monastir, says:—'I am obliged to confess that the people do not appear to have, at present, any confidence in the Government. The chief aim of the Government, therefore, should be to restore that confidence. If their good faith has been doubted, they should seize every opportunity to retrieve their lost character: and without some palpable, earnest, and continued proofs of their good intentions, they can scarcely hope to succeed.' ‡

But this account of the state of alarm under which

* Despatches on apprehended disturbances in Syria, p. 19.
† Ibid. p. 72.
‡ Report of Consuls on Condition of Christians in Turkey, p. 18.

the whole Christian population of this empire drags on its precarious existence would be incomplete without some illustrations of the consequences of the legal disabilities of which the people complain, and to which I trace their discontent more readily than to any hypothetical activity of 'foreign agents.'

I select my illustrations from different parts of Turkey, and the first fact is given on the authority of Mr Calvert, the British consul:—'In June last a Government courier was killed near Maronia, in the pashalic of Salonica, and £2000 was taken from him; the robbery took place just within our frontier. Probably the police-officers of Gallipoli and Serries were, as they generally are, in league with the robbers. Either to screen themselves, or to claim the merit of vigilance and activity, they determined to find the robbers in Maronia. They began by surrounding the village with troops, and for three days they allowed no one to leave it. It was at a critical period of the silkworm harvest. The worms required to be constantly fed with mulberry leaves. The mulberry gardens are out of the village; as no one was allowed to go to them, and fetch leaves, the whole stock of silkworms died. The loss to the village was at least £1500. The police then seized two brothers, Rayahs, respectable men, and accused them of the robbery. The governors of the districts near Maronia came to the village to superintend the investigation, took possession of all the best houses, and lived there with all their retinues at free quarters.

'The brothers proved, or at least offered to prove, an alibi. Many of the principal inhabitants were ready to depose that they had seen the prisoners at the very time of the robbery, and long before and after it, in a coffee-house, in the village. As they were Rayahs, their evidence was rejected.

'"Notwithstanding the Hatt-i-Humáyoon?" I said.

'"The influence," he answered, "of the Hatt-i-Humáyoon does not extend 160 miles from Constantinople."

'To procure evidence against the prisoners by confession, the police proceeded to torture them. One brother could not stand the torture, and confessed the robbery. Then they asked him where the money was; of course he could not tell, so they tortured him again. To obtain a respite, he said that he had hid it in such a place; it was not found there, so the torture was recommenced. He then said that his brother had it. The brother was tortured, but, being more resolute, persisted in his denial.

"You may kill me," he said, "but I will not confess what is not true." This had been going on for some time, the village was almost ruined, both the brothers had been so maimed, that they are cripples for life, when the Pasha of Salonica heard of it, and drew the attention of the Pasha of the Dardanelles to the scenes which were acting by his officers and under his authority. He was indignant, and begged me to assist in the inquiry. It is not quite concluded; but the facts which I have mentioned have come out. I said to the Pasha: "You see now who are the real friends of the Russians. You see what sort of persons and what sort of means are employed to make the Turkish rule hateful to the Christians."'*

Mr Arbuthnot, who accompanied Omer Pasha in his campaign against the people of Herzegovina, and who naturally, from his position, is always inclined to present the Turks in their best aspect, gives us a reason why Bosnia should be discontented. He thus sketches the career of a Turkish pasha, and shows us how a province may be rendered dissatisfied without the aid of foreign intrigues:—'Hadji Ali Pacha commenced his career as a clerk in the pay of the great Mehemet Ali Pacha, Viceroy of Egypt, but,

* Senior, pp. 158, 159.

having deserted to the Turks, he was employed by them in the capacity of Uzbashee or Captain. Fearful of falling into the hands of the Egyptians, he fled from his post, and, having made his way to Constantinople, contrived, by scheming and bribery, not only to efface the memory of the past, but to secure the appointment of Kaimakan or Lieut.-Colonel, with which grade he was sent to Travnik in command of a regiment. Tahir Pacha, the Governor of Bosnia, had about this time been informed of the existence of some gold mines near Travnik, and ordered Hadji Ali to obtain samples for transmission to the Porte. This he did, taking care to retain all the valuable specimens, and forwarding those of inferior quality, which, on their arrival at Constantinople, were declared worthless. No sooner was this decision arrived at, than Hadji Ali imported the necessary machinery and an Austrian mechanic, to separate the gold from the ores, and in this way amassed immense wealth. Rumours having got abroad of what was going on, and the suspicions of Tahir being aroused, the unfortunate Austrian was put secretly out of the way, and, as a blind, the unprincipled ruffian procured the firman to which allusion has been made. It need hardly be said that he never availed himself of the privileges which it conferred upon him. Some time after these transactions, he applied for leave to visit Austria, on the plea of ill-health, but doubtless with the view of changing the gold. This was refused, and he was obliged to employ a Jew, who carried it to Vienna, and disposed of it there. In 1850, when Omer Pacha came to restore order in Bosnia, which had then revolted, Hadji Ali was sent with two battalions to the relief of another detachment; upon this occasion he communicated with the enemy, who cut off his rear-guard, and otherwise roughly handled the Turkish troops. Upon this, Omer Pacha put him in chains, and would have shot him, as he richly deserved, had he not known that his enemies at Constantinople would not fail to distort the true features of the case. He therefore sent him to Constantinople, where he was shortly afterwards released, and employed his gold to such good purpose, that he was actually sent down as Civil Governor to Travnik, which he had so recently left a prisoner convicted of robbery and treason. He was, however, soon dismissed for misconduct, and entered once more into private speculations. In 1857 he purchased the tithes of Bosnia and Herzegovina, and employed such ruffians to collect them as to make perfect martyrs of the people, some of whom were even killed by his agents. Exasperated beyond endurance, the people of Possavina rose *en masse*, and although the movement was put down without difficulty, it doubtless paved the way for the discord and rebellion which has been attended with such calamitous results. This is precisely one of those cases which has brought such odium on the Turkish Government, and which may so easily be avoided for the future, always providing that the Porte be sincere in its oft-repeated protestations of a desire for genuine reform. Ali Pacha was at Mostar in the beginning of 1858, when the movement began, but was afraid to venture into the revolted districts to collect his tithes. The Government, therefore, made him Commandant of the Herzegovinian irregulars, in which post he vindicated the character which he had obtained for cruelty and despotism. Subsequently he was appointed Kaimakan of Trebigné, but the European consuls interfered, and he has now decamped, owing a large sum to Government, the remnant of his contract for the tithes.'*

After reading Lieutenant Arbuthnot's sketch of the career of this pasha, and his remarks upon the effects of the rapacity of such a ruler, the words of

* Herzegovina; or Omer Pacha and the Christian Rebels. By Lieut. G. Arbuthnot, R.H.A. London, 1862.

Mr Zohrab, acting consul at Bosna Serai, acquire additional significance:—'I do not hesitate to say that Bosnia and the Herzegovina, which ought to have been now prosperous, contented, and peaceful, have been turned into discontented, disloyal, poverty-stricken provinces, through the unworthiness of the Sultan's lieutenants, and the gross misconduct of inferior *employés.*'*

How the taxes are collected in this province— how the Christian peasants are oppressed by the subordinates of such a pasha as Hadji Ali—how men are rendered discontented and goaded on to insurrection without the aid of 'foreign intrigues,' may be illustrated by an anecdote related to me by the Princess Julia of Servia:—'The usual method of wringing out the imposts from the Christian peasants in Bosnia is to tie them up in a small apartment and apply fire to green or half-dried wood until the place is filled with smoke. When the Christian is half-suffocated the money is sometimes extracted. Often, however, this fails, for the poor wretch has not sufficient means, and he is left to perish. A short time since a poor widow woman, frantic with agony, burst into the apartments of the Princess

* Report of Consuls on Condition of Christians in Turkey, p. 58.

Julia at the Palace in Belgrade: alternately she wept, imprecated, besought the Princess to redress her wrongs. She had been assessed by the Turkish authorities of a village in Bosnia, on the Servian frontiers, at a sum which she had no more the means of paying than I have of discharging the National Debt. She was smoked. This failed of extracting the gold. She begged for a remission, and stated her inability to pay. In answer she was tossed into the river Drina, and after her were thrown her two infant children, one of four years old, the other of two. Before her eyes, notwithstanding her frantic efforts to save them, her children perished. Half-drowned and insensible, she was dragged to land by a Servian peasant. She made her way to Belgrade, believing, from the character of the Princess for humanity, that if she could she would aid her. Of course to do so was out of the question.'*

Or, to turn in another direction, and to cite another author in illustration of the defenceless condition of which all classes of Christians complain, and which will remain so long as their evidence is refused in a Turkish court of justice, and officials may persecute and torture them with impunity. The relation of this outrage is from the pen of the late

* *The Guardian*, April 29, 1863.

Mr MacFarlane, and, though a few years older than those which I have already given, is but an instance of those wrongs under which these poor people at present groan in all parts of the dominion of the Sultan. It took place after the Tanzimat and the Hatt-i-Humaïoun, and in disregard of all the stipulations which the Government of Turkey had made with the Great Powers of Europe:—' During the late Ramazan Hadji Dhimitri, of Ascià-keui, a picturesque village in the ravine, situated among high rocks, which we had seen on our right hand in coming up from Keuplu to Billijik, had been miserably crippled and otherwise injured by order of the Turkish court, which had let off Abdullah Effendi without so much as a reprimand. Turks as well as Greeks lived at Ascià-keui. One day poor Hadji Dhimitri had with great toil brought up water from a fountain and had filled his reservoir in order to irrigate his little garden and mulberry ground. A Turk, his neighbour, one Kara-Ali, came to him and said that he wanted that water for his own garden and must have it. The Greek said that he might have brought up water for himself, but that he was free to take part of it. The Turk got into a towering passion, called the Greek a ghiaour and pezavenk, and swore he would have all the water. The quarrel was hot, but short. Dhimitri, fearing consequences if he resisted, went away and left the Turk to take and wantonly waste the water, merely saying that he submitted to violence and injustice, and that the Tanzimaut meant nothing. The Turkish savage went to the Mudir and Kadi at Billijik, and vowed that Hadji Dhimitri had wanted to rob him of his water, and had uttered horrible blasphemies against the Koran and the Prophet. Tufekjees were sent to Ascià-keui, and Hadji Dhimitri, being first of all soundly beaten, was handcuffed and chained and brought up to Billijik. The Greeks of the village were afraid of appearing in such a case or against a Mussulman; but four or five did follow the unfortunate Hadji to the hall, misnamed of justice, and were there to depose that it was the Turk who had taken by violence his water and had traduced his religion; and that he, the Hadji, though excited by anger, had not said a word against the Koran or the Prophet. But the testimony of these Christians could not be taken against Mussulman witnesses, and Kara Ali, the Turk, was provided with two false witnesses, one being Shakir Bey, his own son-in-law, and the other Otuz-Bir Oglou-Achmet-Bey. The pair were false witnesses of notoriety, and generally reputed to be the two greatest scoundrels of the town. There were scores upon scores of people who had seen them at the coffee-house in Billijik at the hour and time they pretended to have been at Ascià-kcui, four miles off. But of those who had thus seen them the Mussulmans would not appear, and the Christians could not get their evidence received in court. Kara Ali swore to the truth of his statement; his two false witnesses swore that they had heard the Greek blaspheme their holy religion, and by sentence of the Kadi poor Hadji Dhimitri received, then and there, 300 strokes of the bastinado. His toes were broken by the blows, his feet were beaten to a horrible jelly, he screamed and fainted under the torture. There were some among our narrators who had seen this forbidden torture inflicted, and others who had heard the poor man's shrieks. The victim was carried home on the back of an ass; he had been laid prostrate for more than six weeks; it was only the day before our arrival that he had been able to attend the Billijik market, and then he was lame and sick—a hobbling, crippled, broken man. "The law," said one of our party, " is equal in the two cases. If Hadji Dhimitri were guilty, he was only guilty of that which we have all heard from the lips of Abdullah Effendi this morning in the khan; yet the

Hadji is cruelly bastinadoed and lamed for life, and this same Kadi does not even reprimand the Effendi. What then is the use of this Tanzimaut?" "The use of it," said Tchelebee John, "is just this: it throws dust in the eyes of the foreign ambassadors at Constantinople who recommended its promulgation, and it humbugs half the nations of Christendom, where people believe in newspaper reports."'*

I add one other illustration of the way in which discontent and dissatisfaction are fostered, not by 'foreign intrigues,' but by the misgovernment of the Sultan. The narrative is one which I have already made use of in my little volume on Servia. I reproduce it in preference to many other similar anecdotes which I might have given, for the same reason which led me to print it before. It was related to me by a consul and his wife, who both witnessed the act of atrocity. I recorded it immediately after leaving their house. In one only part of it I have intentionally spoken vaguely. I have no wish to draw down upon their heads the wrath of Sir Henry Bulwer; I have not, therefore, indicated the exact place where it happened, lest I should betray my informants:—'A short

* Destiny of Turkey, by Chas. MacFarlane, vol. i. pp. 336—338.

time since the inhabitants of a little village in Roumelia were called upon to pay the taxes, at which they had been assessed by the authorities of the district in which the village is situated. When the principal inhabitants had assembled, they did what probably many others would have done in like circumstances, they rather discussed the means by which the tax might be evaded than the mode of paying it. After many schemes had been suggested, the only means which appeared satisfactory to those who were present, was to compel some inhabitant who was not present to pay the whole assessment. In the outskirts of the village resided a Christian peasant, who owned a small strip of ground, which he cultivated for his maintenance. He was industrious, and was supposed to possess a hoard of money. Indeed, as he had only one child—a son who assisted him in the cultivation of his rood of land—how could he spend all his earnings? It was evident, so his Mussulman neighbours argued, there must be a store somewhere, and it was resolved that he should be compelled to pay the whole amount at which the village was assessed. By this means it was clear that the claim of the Porte would be satisfied, and the rest of the villagers would be lightened from the burden about to be imposed upon them. The discussion took place in the presence of the cadi. He assured the assembly that it was a matter of indifference how the money was procured, provided that it was duly paid to him. After some deliberation as to the best means of wringing the whole sum from one peasant, the following plan was suggested, matured, and finally carried out. It was agreed that the rest of the villagers should seize his only child, a lad of some sixteen years, and imprison him until his father should ransom him for the sum at which the whole village was assessed; and that the cadi should suspend the collection of the tax until this means had been tried. In order that this functionary should not, however, pocket the ransom himself, and then levy the tax upon the villagers, a deed was drawn up and witnessed according to the forms of Turkish law, by which the cadi covenanted to accept the money thus to be wrung from the parent in lieu of all claim upon the rest of the villagers; to hold the boy in his custody until the ranson should be paid, and to release him as soon as this should be done. It was seed-time, and the lad, wholly unconscious of the plot, was employed with his parents in ploughing and sowing their little piece of ground, when he was seized, carried off to the cadi, and, amidst the cries of his mother and the entreaties of his father, thrown into prison, with the intimation that he should be released when the money was paid. The village was but ill-supplied with prison buildings, and the boy was thrust into the small dome, of some six feet square, which covered an unused well. Day by day the parents came, but could not weary the patience of the unjust but impassive judge. The only answer which they received was, that when the money was brought the boy should be released. The parents were not wealthy; they had no hoard; the supposition of their fellow-villagers was unfounded; they had nothing save the small strip of land which they cultivated for their daily needs. The last thing which a peasant will give up in Turkey is the privilege of being a landed proprietor. The father, who loved his son, clung, however, to his bit of garden ground, and exhausted all other means of raising the required sum before selling his land. He appealed to the authorities of the district. He was referred by them for redress to the cadi, by whom the wrong was done. Despairing of any other means of delivering his child, the wretched parents now endeavoured to collect the money which the cadi required. Their furniture was first sold, then their tools and implements of husbandry were parted with. The sum thus obtained fell so far short of the amount required, that it was at length evident that the rood of ground, the family estate, must be parted with. This also was sold, and still there lacked a portion of the total sum required. The cadi was inexorable, and rigidly upright. The Government expected so much from the village, and so much must be brought before the lad could be released. At length the last piastre was procured, and the wretched parents hastened joyfully to the cadi with the whole amount. All this had taken upwards of ten months to collect, and for so long a time the poor lad had been subjected to the horrors of solitary confinement, in total darkness, and in a dungeon only a few feet in extent, in which it was impossible to stand upright. The floor, partly of rough stones and partly of mud, was equally cold and damp, and on this he had sat and lain and lain and sat for more than ten months. On receiving the money the cadi assembled the villagers; the deed was recited; the money exhibited, and the legal instrument duly cancelled with all the mocking formalities of law. And now the prison door, or what served for a door, was unbarred to the parents, and they were permitted to look again upon their child. For a time nothing moved within the narrow limits of the cell; the call of his mother could elicit no signs of life in the poor prisoner. At length a bundle of humanity was dragged out; it breathed; it stirred: but these were the only tokens of life which could be seen. Signs of humanity there were none. The limbs had been contracted by cold, wet, rheumatism, and by the crouching posture which the poor lad had been compelled to assume, and he could only crawl on all-fours like a beast. His face resembled a skull covered with dirty parchment, and he was hopelessly an idiot. How long since reason had given way his jailors could not tell. He was now a slobbering, jabbering idiot. The light, and joy, and hope of his parents' cottage was not merely quenched, it had become a palpable and noisome blackness.

'Amidst the wails of the parents, and the "God is great" of the persecutors, the crowd dispersed, some cursing more deeply than ever the despotism which rendered them liable to atrocities such as these. It needs no "Russian intrigues" to make these poor peasants believe that deeds like these are unjust, and to inspire them with a longing for an opportunity to break such an intolerable yoke from their necks. For this incident is but a specimen of what the Christians throughout Bosnia, Roumelia, and Bulgaria are now enduring. I could narrate acts of atrocious cruelty and wrong which would go far beyond this; but I have selected this anecdote because I can tell it on other authority than that of a Servian or a Dalmatian. I did not hear it from a suffering, and therefore a "prejudiced, Bosniac" or a "lying Greek." Amongst the crowd which witnessed this horror, amongst the many who saw the shattered remains of this poor and innocent lad dragged forth from his cell, and handed to his parents by the cadi, were the British consul and his wife, and from their lips I heard this tale of barbarity.' *

But beyond the unexceptionable nature of the source from which I obtained this illustration of the way in which a Turkish province is governed, and our Christian brethren are oppressed, I have reprinted this anecdote because, subsequently to its original publication, I have submitted it to persons conversant, from long residence, with the actual state of the Turkish empire, and I am assured that similar atrocities happen in every province, in every district, of that country, so that this fairly represents the normal condition of our brethren unhappily living under the rule of the Sultan.†

* Servia and the Servians, pp. 288—292.
† See in the second volume of Mr MacFarlane's 'Turkey and its Destiny,' pp. 1—8, a somewhat similar story of exaction and wrong.

Here are, surely, sufficient elements to produce discontent amongst the Christians of Turkey without our having recourse to any imaginary amount of 'foreign intrigues,' or of clandestine exertions of 'Russian agents.' If, indeed, weighed down by these intolerable severities, they do turn at times to some one who can protect them against their cruel oppressors, it is not a matter for wonder. They have ceased to expect anything, except additional wrongs, from their rulers. Husbands and fathers as they are, and unarmed in the midst of an armed Mussulman population, they must look to some one to interpose in their behalf. At present this takes the form of supplicating passports from English, French, and, less frequently, from Russian consuls, so as to avail themselves of their protection; and, while their condition is such as the illustrations which I have just given reveal to us, they will look for protection to any quarter of the heavens where there is the least gleam of sympathy, the least break in the dark cloud which hangs so heavily over them. That they do so—that they must do so—is the severest condemnation of the Government of the Sultan.

Mr Abbott, the consul at the Dardanelles, says, that the 'vexatious and arbitrary proceedings of Turkish officials' is the cause why 'the subjects of

the Porte get foreign passports,' and, after recounting a narrative of petty oppression, he tells us:—
'It is not a matter for surprise in the face of similar facts, which are of daily occurrence, that the Rayahs should occasionally resort to the only means at hand of protecting themselves against the shortcomings of their legitimate rulers; and it is the greatest reproach upon the Turkish Government, as well as one of the most incontestable proofs of its weak and degenerate state, that its own subjects should be compelled in self-defence to throw off their lawful allegiance, inasmuch as they are denied the protection which they have a right to expect, and are less favoured in this respect than foreigners; being the reverse of what occurs in civilized countries.

'When a foreign passport cannot be procured, the Rayahs find it advantageous to carry on business in ostensible partnership with a foreigner or under a foreigner's power of attorney. This affords a great security for their property, and has become a common practice.

'This anomalous state of things will not cease to exist, until the Porte has completed the task of reforming the present defective administration of justice, and has provided for that purpose properly-

FOREIGN INTRIGUES. 115

constituted tribunals. When that time arrives, the Rayahs will, I doubt not, cheerfully return to their allegiance.' *

Unhappily, as the evidence of the consuls show, the sufferings of the Christians throughout Turkey, so far from diminishing, are actually increasing. The legal condition of the Christian is as degraded as ever. The text-books of the law, by which the decisions of the cadi are regulated, are as intolerant as ever. It is easy to profess incredulity on this matter; it is not so easy to overcome the logic of facts. The Multka is still the authority to which all Mussulmans appeal throughout Turkey. It is a book which possesses an authority greater than that of Lyndewood in our ecclesiastical tribunals. It ranks higher than Coke or Blackstone do in our common law courts; and the precedents and axioms of this book of Institutes of Mahommedan law are not only still used and cited, but the volume is the ruling authority of the court of Turkey, from which no one dreams of appealing. In that book we read, and, more still, every cadi reads:—' And the tributary (or Christian) is to be distinguished in the beast he rides, and in his saddle, and he is not to

* Report of Consuls on Condition of Christians in Turkey, p. 88.

ride a horse, he is not to work at his work with arms on, he shall not ride on a saddle like a pillion, he shall not ride on that except as a matter of necessity, and even then he shall dismount in places of public resort; he shall not wear clothes worn by men of learning, piety, and nobility. His women shall be distinguished in the street and at the baths, and he shall place in his house a sign and mark so that people may not pray for him or salute him. And the street shall be narrowed for him, and he shall pay his tribute standing, the receiver being seated, and he shall be seized by the collar, and shall be shaken, and it shall be said to him, "Pay the tribute, oh, tributary! oh, thou enemy of God!"'*

Nor are the forms of Turkish law, even when

---

* The Multka, or digest of the Mahometan Canon Law, from which this extract is made, was written in Arabic by a Turkish lawyer several centuries ago. It gives the decisions arrived at by the two great legists of Sunni Mahommedanism, and is the text-book and authority in the law courts throughout Turkey. Indeed, all Sunni legists in Turkey, and in other Sunni countries, study this book, and make their references to it. Cadis and Muftis take it, with other similar books, as a guide to their decisions, as our judges consult the decisions of their predecessors. It is, however, of a far greater authority than any such decisions can be amongst ourselves; because it is a fundamental principle in Turkey that no one, neither the Sultan nor the government combined, can change or abrogate the Canon Law of that country.

the spirit has grown more tolerant, one whit more favourable to the poor Rayahs. Persecuted in life, 'treated,' as long as they lived, 'not merely as slaves, but as slaves whom their masters hate,' * the persecution, the hatred, the contempt goes with them to their grave. In his account of the siege of Kars, Dr Sandwith has printed a burial certificate which is given when a Christian dies.† It is in these terms :—

'*We certify to the priest of the church of Mary, that the impure, putrified, stinking carcase of Saideh, damned this day, may be concealed under-ground.*
  '*Sealed.*   EL SAID MEHEMED FAIZI.
'A.H. 1271.   *Rejib* 11.'
(*March* 29, A.D. 1855.)

What years of hatred must have been endured before the feeling was embodied in this document! What years of hatred must have been endured since! How deep the scorn, how bitter the contempt, how fierce the intolerance! So long as, even in official forms, such words as these are used, what hope can there be for a great part of the unhappy subjects of this empire?

* Senior, p. 113.　　　† Siege of Kars, p. 173.

CHAPTER V.

TURKISH PROMISES AND TURKISH NON-PERFORMANCES.

IN order to abate the wrongs of which the Christians of Turkey have long complained, the Great Powers of Europe have, from time to time, insisted upon certain concessions being made to them in return for the material assistance which the Western Powers have granted, the blood so lavishly poured out, the treasure so freely expended. They demanded in 1839, and again on the non-fulfilment of that demand, in 1856, on the termination of the war with Russia, certain stipulations, of which these are the principal: (1) That the evidence of Christians should be received by the Turkish courts of justice equally with that of Mussulmans. They pressed this the more earnestly since it is evident without this neither life nor property is secure. (2) That the Christian peasant should be able to purchase and hold land, and should not be liable to be ousted from his possession at the caprice of his Mahommedan neighbour. (3) That in regulating the taxation of the empire, Mahommedans and Christians should be placed in a position of equality. (4) That both races should be eligible to serve in the army, and that it should be as lawful for the Christian to possess arms as the Mussulman. (5) That compulsory conversion to the Mahommedan faith should be abolished.

Every one of these essential conditions to the freedom of the Christian races of Turkey remains, however, notwithstanding repeated pledges, as much disregarded as they were fifty years ago. On this head let me cite the words of Lord Derby, who thus describes the Andrassy proposals for the quieting of the Herzegovina. They sum up the faithlessness of 'our faithful ally.' 'The proposals of Count Andrassy amount to little more than a request that the Porte will execute the Hatti-Scheriff of Gulhané of 1839, the Hatti-Humayoun of 1856, and the Iradé and Firman of the 2nd October and 12th of December last; in short, that the measures for the improvement of the condition of the non-Mussulman and rural population generally throughout the empire, which have been publicly proclaimed, should be brought into practical application.'* In a word, that the solemn promise made to the Great Powers of Europe nearly forty years ago should now be performed, or, in Lord Derby's phrase, be 'brought into practical application;' but to particularize:—

(1) The evidence of a Christian is not received either in the criminal or civil courts of Turkey. It is true that some shadow of equality in this respect, between the Mussulman and non-Mussulman, exists at Constantinople, and is ostentatiously pointed out to travellers who limit their observations to that capital. But this only makes the faithlessness of Turkey to treaties the more evident.

In the Hatt-i-Sherif of 1856, the Sultan, at the pressing instance of the European Powers, decreed:— 'The guarantees promised on our part by the Hatt-i-Humaïoun of Gul-Hané, and in conformity with the Tanzimat, to all the subjects of my Empire, without distinction of classes or of religion, for the security of their persons and property, and the preservation of their honour, are to-day confirmed and consolidated, and efficacious measures shall be taken in order that they may have their full and entire effect.' . . .

* Correspondence respecting Affairs in Bosnia and in Herzegovina, 1876.

'All commercial, correctional, and criminal suits between Mussulmans and Christian or other non-Mussulman subjects, or between Christians or other non-Mussulmans of different sects, shall be referred to Mixed Tribunals.

'The proceedings of these tribunals shall be public; the parties shall be confronted, and shall produce their witnesses, whose testimony shall be received, without distinction, upon an oath taken according to the religious law of each sect.'

It must be observed that the Sultan here appeals to a former promise made to the same effect as the provisions of the Hatt-i-Sherif; the Hatt-i-Humaïoun to which he refers bears date Nov. 3, 1839, and even this latter was only in accordance with the Tanzimat still more remote in date, so that, when it is pleaded by the Sultan's advocates that, though the Hatt-i-Sherif has been entirely disregarded, yet that this was only promised six years ago, and if we have patience its provisions may yet be carried out; this is said in ignorance of the real circumstances of the case. The pledge that Christian evidence shall be received in the courts of justice throughout Turkey, and be accepted on the same footing as Mahometan evidence, was made upwards of thirty years ago.*

* Now, alas! fifty years ago.

How then has this pledge, made to the nations of Europe, and re-confirmed in consideration of the blood poured out and the treasure expended by the Allied Powers in behalf of Turkey, been fulfilled?

The seventh question in the list forwarded by Sir Henry Bulwer to the 'Consuls in the Ottoman dominions,' was as follows :—'Is Christian evidence admitted in courts of justice; and if not, point out the cases where it has been refused?'*

In answer to this, Mr Abbott, the English consul at Monastir, writes:—'It is only admitted at the Tahkik Medjlis (Court of Inquiry). There, Christian witnesses are sworn, whereas Mussulmans are not. I cannot point out cases where it has been refused at the other Courts, as, it being considered an established rule not to admit Christian evidence, a Christian has never dared present in a suit one of his co-religionists to give his testimony.' †

To the same inquiry Mr Finn, the consul at Jerusalem, thus replies :—'In the Mehkemeh, or Cadi's Court, non-Mussulman evidence is always refused. In the various Medjlises some subterfuge is always sought for declining to receive non-Mussulman evidence against a Mussulman, or recording it

* Report of Consuls on the Condition of the Christians in Turkey, p. 3. † Ibid. p. 7.

under the technical name of witness. These Courts and the Pasha will rather condemn at once a Mussulman in favour of a Christian, without recording testimony, than accept non-Moslem evidence. Evidence of Christian against Christian, or Jew, or *vice versa*, *i.e.* non-Moslem against non-Moslem, is always received.' *

Mr J. E. Blunt, consul at Pristina:—'Christian evidence in law-suits between a Mussulman and a non-Mussulman is not admitted in the local Courts.

'In such cases in which the parties are not Mussulman, Christian evidence is admitted.' †

Mr Skene, the consul at Aleppo, in his report, says:—'It is not admitted; and the attempt is never made to obtain its admission. No case has occurred in connection with the business of this consulate to raise the question.' ‡

Major Cox, the consul at Bucharest, says:—'In cases between Christians, yes; but in cases between Christians and Mahometans, no. This is one of the subjects on which the intelligent portion of the Christians earnestly insist for redress, and which they know at the same time is one of the most difficult for the Ottoman Government to deal with, on

* Report of Consuls on the Condition of the Christians in Turkey, p. 27. † Ibid. p. 35. ‡ Ibid. p. 50.

account of the strong prejudices entertained by the Mussulmans.'*

Other consuls, indeed, report that the evidence of Christians is received in the criminal courts of justice in certain provinces of Turkey, but when we come to examine in what way it is received we find that contrary assertions are not always contradictory.

Mr Charles Blunt, of Smyrna, thus answers Sir Henry Bulwer's question :—'Generally speaking, from all that I can learn, Christian evidence is not admitted against Mussulmans in the interior, but only one instance has been brought before me, which was in 1857, when the authorities at Aidin would not admit Christian evidence in a suit in which a British subject was interested. On that occasion, in conjunction with the Pasha of Smyrna, officers were sent from the Governor and this Consulate to Aidin, when upon their united interference Christian evidence was, and has since been, admitted in the courts of Aidin. [Christian evidence is admitted in the courts at Smyrna, but in all suits relating to houses and landed property, foreign Christian evidence is not admitted against the native Christian.'†

---

* Report of Consuls on the Condition of the Christians in Turkey, p. 58. The 'difficulty' has now been dealt with and overcome ; but then Bucharest is the capital of an autonomous state. † Ibid. p. 32.

Mr Cathcart, the consul at Prevesa, states:—
'Christian evidence is always admitted in the courts of justice, but I think it doubtful whether, in cases between a Mussulman and a Christian, it carries the same weight as Mahometan evidence.'*

Acting-Consul Zohrab, writing from Bosna Serai, says:—'Christian evidence in the Medjlises is occasionally received, but as a rule it is refused, either directly or indirectly, by reference to the Mehkemeh. Knowing this, the Christians generally come forward prepared with Mussulman witnesses. The cases in which Christian evidence has been refused are numerous, but it would take time to collect them.'†

Mr Moore, the consul at Beyrout, writes:—
'Christian evidence is admitted into the mixed Tribunals (those composed of Christian and Mussulman members), but not in the purely Turkish court called the Mehkemeh, or in the Grand Medjlis of the Eyalet when it is presided over by the Cadi, and where the law may be administered according to the Sharâ (Mahometan Ecclesiastical law). *In case of murder, for instance, when the murderer is a Moslem, that presidency and that law are resorted to, and Chris-*

* Report of Consuls on the Condition of the Christians in Turkey, p. 42. † Ibid. p. 55.

tian evidence would be rejected. No such case having occurred for many years, I am unable to furnish instances. Petty criminal cases are tried at the Medjlis Tahkik (Court of Verification), and civil suits at the Commercial Courts, both mixed Tribunals where Christian evidence is accepted.' *

Mr Abbott, the consul at the Dardanelles, says:— 'It is admitted; though, generally speaking, the testimony of a Mussulman carries with it more weight. I may here add, that circumstantial evidence, though of the clearest nature, is refused; that the Tidjaret-Medjlis, or Commercial Tribunal, goes only upon documentary evidence; that the testimony of one female is rejected as insufficient, whilst that of two females, of whatever creed, is accepted, being considered equivalent to that of one male. Owing to these peculiarities of Turkish law, a miscarriage of justice often ensues: whilst the fear of incurring vengeance deters many persons, both Mussulmans and Christians, from prosecuting notorious malefactors, or giving evidence against them.' †

Major Cox, again writing from Bucharest, says: —' The non-reception of the testimony of Christians on the same footing with that of the Mussulmans is

* Report of Consuls on the Condition of the Christians in Turkey, p. 71. † Ibid. p. 70.

as much a subject of complaint in Bosnia and the Herzegovine as in Bulgaria.' *

In order in some degree to protect Christian witnesses, the Porte consented to the appointment of Christian assessors in the Medjlises, or local courts. This has been carried out certainly in form, though in substance the stipulation is as much disregarded as that by which the testimony of a Christian was declared to be placed on the same footing as that of a Mussulman.

Mr Calvert, the consul at Monastir, tells us :— 'As to the Christian members, they take their seats at the Medjlises as a matter of form, but dare not dissent from an opinion emitted by the Mussulman members. I hear that, some years back, the Christian member of the Medjlis at Monaster was poisoned for opposing his Mussulman colleagues.' †

To the same purpose Mr Calvert, writing from Salonica, says :—' Christians are admitted into the local Councils, but they are so few in number compared with the Mussulman members as to be completely overawed, and therefore practically useless. They blindly affix their seals to the "Mazbattas" (reports or decisions) which are written in Turkish,

* Report of Consuls on the Condition of the Christians in Turkey, p. 96.   † Ibid. p. 4.

—a language they can rarely read; and even were they to understand what was written, they would scarcely venture to refuse to confirm it, although they might inwardly dissent from the purport of the document.'*

I content myself with citing only one other witness, Mr Finn, the consul at Jerusalem:— 'Christians are admitted as members of the Medjlises by virtue of laws of the Central Government, but the number of the members proportioned to the number of the sect is not equal to the proportion of the Mussulman members to the number of their sect. For instance, the Jews, who nearly equal the Christians and Mussulmans together, have but one member in each Medjlis; the Christians, who are nearly equal to the Mussulmans, have but one member of each sect in each Medjlis; while the Mussulman members are as numerous as the Pasha pleases to make them,—generally six or seven.'

'They are barely tolerated by the Mussulman members, and are always placed in lower seats: they have not the courage to make use of the privileges as intended. I sometimes hear of their placing

* Report of Consuls on the Condition of the Christians in Turkey, p. 12.

their seals falsely to Mazbattas, merely from fear of displeasing the Mussulman members.' *

Now, so long as this is the case—so long as Christian evidence is wholly refused, or is not allowed to have any weight in the determination of a civil suit, whilst it is utterly rejected in all criminal causes, it is obvious there can be no security for life, limb, nor property for the great mass of the Christian subjects of the Sultan. Murder, attended by the most revolting circumstances, and perpetrated in the midst of a crowded Christian village, and in the sight of a hundred witnesses, is never punished, because the evidence of all these people is inadmissible in the courts of Turkey. What impunity this gives to the criminal, and what encouragement to the commission of outrages, must be evident to every one.

From a report of Mr Finn, dated Jerusalem, January 4, 1860, we obtain a glimpse of the normal condition of the Turkish provinces, as to the administration of justice :—'The Arabs have a proverb that the Divine Government acts upon the two motives of, first, reward ; secondly, punishment ; but that in

* Report of Consuls on the Condition of the Christians in Turkey, p. 28.

Turkish rule it is all Heaven, there is no penalty for transgression.

'On this same principle, political rebels are at the most only disabled temporarily from doing mischief. Officers of regiments convicted of extortion and peculation are only removed from one station to another. *Pashas (with but one exception that I have known) are always promoted, when dismissed on the complaints of consuls; and throughout my experience I have never known a robbery or other such offence punished as a crime.* When burglars or highway robbers are discovered and convicted, it is always considered an ample retribution if a sum almost amounting to the loss is levied upon the guilty. The Government congratulates itself and the plaintiff on the success obtained, but the criminality is never punished.*

When this is the case with reference to all crime, except in rare and exceptional cases, it is not surprising that crimes against Christians are committed with total impunity.

Mr J. E. Blunt, of Pristina, thus reports three cases which had occurred in his neighbourhood:—

---

* Despatches on apprehended disturbances in Syria, 1858 —1860, p. 90.

'About seventeen months ago a Turkish soldier murdered a Mahometan, an old man, who was working in his field. The only persons, two in number, who witnessed the deed are Christians. The Medjlis of Uscup would not take their evidence, although the Undersigned urged the Kaimakam to accept it.

'About the same time a Zaptieh tried by force to convert a Bulgarian girl to Islamism. As she declared before the Medjlis of Camanova that she would not abjure her religion, he killed her in the very precincts of the Mudir's house. This tragedy created great sensation in the province. The Medjlises of Camanova and Prisrend would not accept Christian evidence, and every effort was made to save the Zaptieh; but on the case being referred to Constantinople, an order reached the authorities to "take the evidence of all persons who witnessed the murder." This was done, and Kiani Pasha, who at the time took charge of the province, where he has done much good, immediately had the Zaptieh beheaded.

'Six months ago a Bulgarian in the district of Camanova was attacked, without provocation on his part, by two Albanians. They wounded him severely.

On the case being referred to Prisrend, the Medjlis refused to take cognizance of it, as the only evidence produced was Christian.' *

To this I would add an extract from Dr Sandwith's account of his travels in Armenia:—' An Armenian tradesman, about to leave the town [of B—] for another city, had been trying to change some paper-money into gold, the former not being current at the place of his destination. An officer, hearing of this, went and offered the Armenian gold for 5000 piastres in paper (about 40*l.*), ten per cent. agio being deducted. This offer the Armenian accepted, and gave the officer the paper-money, the latter promising to return immediately with the gold. Some time having elapsed, and the officer not having made his appearance, the Armenian went to look after him, and with much trouble succeeded in recovering, at various instalments, 4060 piastres. The Armenian then applied to the Turk's commanding officer for the payment of the remainder, who recommended that the affair should be taken to the mijlis. The Turk, seeing that the proofs were rather strong against him, insisted on his right to be tried by the mehkémé, where he knew that the Koran

* Report of Consuls on the Condition of Christians in Turkey, pp. 35, 36.

would serve him in his need. Accordingly the Armenian and the Turk were confronted before this religious tribunal; and there the Turk, grown bold, as a Mussulman, declared that, far from owing the Armenian anything, the latter wished to rob him; that he (the Turk) had placed the above-named sum in the hands of a third person to be changed into gold, and that the Armenian had taken it for that purpose, but that the gold was not forthcoming. "Do you swear to this?" asked the President. "I swear it on the Koran," answered the Turk. "It is enough." The Armenian had brought witnesses, but they were all Christians, their evidence was impossible; so the hapless Armenian was obliged to refund all the gold he had previously obtained, and found himself a ruined man.' *

The consequence of this impunity is murder on so large a scale as almost to amount to continuous massacre. Thus, Mr Rogers, the vice-consul at Beyrout, reports from information satisfactory to himself:—

'*Exclusive of the blood shed in open civil warfare between the years* 1841 *and* 1858, *or in other words, during the space of seventeen years,* 780 *individual murders have been committed in Mount Lebanon; and*

* Narrative of the Siege of Kars, pp. 169, 170.

probably since the year 1858 *upwards of* 300 *more have occurred, thus forming a total of about* 1100 *in the space of nineteen years, not one of which has been avenged by law.**

In illustration of what Mr Rogers here states the following details of such unprovoked, unpunished murders occur in Mr Evans' recent volume of travels —' As we were walking our engineer pointed to a part of a maize plot on the road-side where the maize was slightly trodden down. "Do you see that?" he asked; "perhaps you would like to know how the maize got trodden down there?" He then recounted to us the following narrative, which, coming from an eye-witness, served to enlighten us considerably about the amenities of Turkish rule. It must be prefaced that at the present time no one can go from one village to another without being provided with a Turkish pass, and that it was one of the practices of the Belgian engineer, as head of the road commission, to examine and set his *vizé* on the pass of all who passed along the road. A few days ago a young Herzegovinian Christian stopped at his tent and showed his pass, which proved to be quite *en règle*, and was *vizéd* by the engineer accordingly. He then proceeded on his way with a light heart, but as

* Correspondence on Affairs of Syria, 1860, 1861, p. 404.

he was passing by the booths near the bridge, two Turks—not officials or soldiers of any kind, but armed nevertheless—came up and insolently demanded to see his pass. This they had not a shadow of a right to ask for; but the young fellow, knowing that in this country might is right, did not hesitate to comply, and handed his pass for their examination. Thereupon the two Mahometans, who could not read a syllable, swore that the whole thing was wrong, and seizing hold of the young rayah, began to drag him along, crying out to the Christians that they were taking him off to the road commission. But they had not proceeded far when they suddenly fell upon him, and hauling him off into the maize, butchered him with severe blows from their *handshars*, one of which half cut through his neck. They then made off in broad daylight, making their way through the Christians and others, whom the young fellow's cries were bringing to the scene of the tragedy—not a Greek daring to lay hands on the murderers, who were Turks. The Belgian who was in his tent had been roused by a loud "*Homaun! homaun!*" as he expressed the cries, and coming out found the young rayah, who had succeeded in crawling to the road, past human assistance.'* Do

* Through Bosnia and Herzegovina, p. 313.

people thus treated, thus exposed by Turkish law to outrage and murder, need 'Servian agitators' or 'Russian agents' to teach them that they are foully wronged, or to inspire them with hatred towards their 'paternal Government'?

I have dwelt at length on the refusal of Christian evidence in the Turkish courts of law, because it is the fountain of that injustice of which these people complain. From this flows, as from a copious wellhead, impunity for every outrage which the malice of envious neighbours, the cupidity of greedy officials, and the lustfulness of casual travellers of the ruling race, can prompt. Throughout the whole extent of the Turkish empire, every young girl, every Christian wife, is the lawful prey of any wandering Mussulman, who is at perfect liberty, in wantonness or in the consciousness of power, to show his contempt for the sanctities of a Christian household by the violation of any or every member of it, and the father, husband, or brother are liable to punishment, even that of death, if they defend their own honour and that of the females of their family. Well may Mr Layard say—'Wherever the Osmanli has placed his foot he has bred fear and distrust. His visit has been one of oppression and rapine. The scarlet cap and the well-known garb of a Turkish irregular are the signals for a general panic. The women hide themselves in the innermost recesses to save themselves from insult; the men slink into their houses, and offer a vain protest against the seizure of their property.'

Even Mr Longworth, the consul-general at Belgrade, and formerly consul at Monastir, says, 'The forcible abduction of Christian girls by Mahometans is an abuse which calls urgently for correction.' * . . . There is, however, but little prospect that this abuse will be corrected, since Mr Abbott tells us—' A custom prevails here to exempt from military conscription a Mussulman young man who elopes with a Christian girl, and whom he converts to his faith. This being considered a meritorious act for his religion, it entitles him, as a reward, to be freed from military service.'†

When a man can, by the laws of Turkey, avoid the conscription merely by seizing and violating a Christian girl, it is not to be wondered if such cases abound in this ill-fated country. Nor is the singular provision, that he should convert to his own 'faith' the victim of his lust, any safeguard to a Christian maiden, since, if she appeals to the tribu-

* Consular Reports on the Condition of Christians in Turkey, p. 21. † Ibid. p. 7.

nals, she is utterly unable to obtain redress: should she declare herself a Mahometan, then the ravisher is held to have done a praiseworthy action; should she proclaim herself a Christian, she is, by the law of Turkey, prohibited from giving evidence of the wrong done to her; so that, in either case, she must submit. On the subject Mr Longworth, apologizing as he does for Turkish abuses, yet says—'It is an old custom of these wild districts, and was formerly held to evince manly spirit on the part of the ravisher. It is asserted also, and I believe it, that the girls are frequently consenting parties to their own abduction, and that the parents, by delaying to give them in marriage, with a view of appropriating their services as long as possible, indirectly bring this misfortune on themselves. But these palliatives, and others of the kind, which may be urged, are, I think, beside the question, which is simply if seduction and violence has been employed in removing these girls from the roof and protection of their parents. But instead of putting it to this issue, it has been the rule to force the party to appear before the tribunal which rejects Christian evidence, and to dispose of the affair summarily, by compelling her to declare herself a Christian or a Mahometan.' *

* Consular Reports on the Condition of Christians in Turkey, p. 21.

(2) Where the safety of life and respect for the honour of the family is utterly disregarded, it is not to be expected that much consideration will be given to the rights of property. With reference to this particular, the injustice and cruelty of their Turkish masters press heavily upon the whole Christian population. Acts of oppression, incited by the desire to possess the property of the subject race, will, indeed, be more numerous than murders and deeds of violence to Christian women, since cupidity is a more universal passion amongst men than even the thirst for blood or the gratification of lust.

This fact has not escaped the attention of the Powers of Europe. So far indeed as solemn stipulations can go, nothing at present can be desired in behalf of the Christian subjects of the Porte. But then it must be remembered that every stipulation made has been—I will not say broken, because that implies a state of things which has existed and been violently destroyed—but disregarded. It must be borne in mind that no treaty has, on this point, ever been fulfilled. Every promise has been forgotten. Whenever a loan is required, for which the guarantee of England is necessary, or the assistance of this country is desired for the preservation of 'the integrity of Turkey,' and the lives of our fellow-countrymen are to be sacrificed on her soil, or the industry of England weighed down by taxation imposed for the security of the Ottoman power, we have promises in abundance—the Hatt-i-Sherifs and Hatt-i-Humaïouns, which are then drawn up and signed, bristle with the pledges of freedom. But the loan once obtained, the assistance once given, the money squandered, and the blood of Englishmen poured out beyond recall; every pledge is broken, every treaty forgotten, and the Hatt-i-Humaïoun, which has declared the equality of the Mussulmans and Christians of Turkey in the eyes of the law, is quietly withdrawn. No nation, except Turkey, has ever shown such a flagrant disregard, such a contempt, for public treaties. Where the rights of her Christian subjects are concerned no attempt is ever made to observe them. Nor can this be said to be of little moment to ourselves. We are concerned in this breach of faith, we are parties to it. The simple right which the Christians of Turkey claim, the right to be heard as witnesses when the blood of their brothers has been shed in their sight, when their wives and daughters have been outraged, is one which we have pledged ourselves to procure for them; the right of the Christian to hold property has been demanded as the price of our assistance in upholding the rule of the Sultan. Neither right has been conceded, neither promise has been fulfilled, and we go on murmuring and maundering about 'the integrity of Turkey;' but we are utterly indifferent whether Turkey takes any steps to preserve her own 'integrity,' by performing the repeated promises made on this subject, or whether she destroys the one and violates the other by her faithlessness.

In the negotiations preceding the treaty of Paris, the condition of the Christians of Turkey engaged the attention of the representatives of the great European Powers. In order to obtain some guarantee that the Sultan would no longer disregard the provisions solemnly promised by the Hatt-i-Humaïoun of Gul-Hané of 1839, which itself, however, as I have before said, was only a reiteration of like promises made in the Tanzimat of an older date, it was proposed that stipulations for the rights of the Christian people of Turkey should form a part of the treaty to be signed at Paris. At the representation, however, of the Turkish minister that the Sultan would prefer to issue a document for this purpose, as though it were his own free act and not part of the proceedings of the Congress then assembled, this was overruled, and accordingly the

treaty of Paris was completed without any stipulations for the better treatment of the Christians. It was left to the Sultan's honour, and the only notice taken of the subject, is that contained in the Ninth Article of the treaty, which is in these words:—
'His Imperial Majesty the Sultan, having, in his constant solicitude for the welfare of his subjects, issued a firman which, while ameliorating their condition without distinction of religion or of race, records his generous intentions towards the Christian population of his Empire, and wishing to give a further proof of his sentiments in that respect, has resolved to communicate to the Contracting Parties the said firman, emanating spontaneously from his sovereign will.' *

A few weeks before this treaty was signed, the Sultan had issued his Hatt-i-Sherif, in which he says :—' The guarantees promised on our part by the Hatt-i-Humaïoun of Gul-Hané, and in conformity with the Tanzimat, to all the subjects of my Empire, without distinction of classes or of religion, for the security of their persons and property and the preservation of their honour, are to-day confirmed and consolidated, and efficacious measures shall be taken

* Treaty of Paris. Parliamentary Paper, p. 20.

in order that they may have their full and entire effect.'

* * * * * *

'The equality of taxes entailing equality of burdens, as equality of duties entails that of rights, Christian subjects, and those of other non-Mussulman sects, as it has been already decided, shall, as well as Mussulmans, be subject to the obligations of the Law of Recruitment. The principle of obtaining substitutes, or of purchasing exemption, shall be admitted. A complete law shall be published, with as little delay as possible, respecting the admission into and service in the army of Christian and other non-Mussulman subjects.'

* * * * * *

'The taxes are to be levied under the same denomination from all the subjects of my Empire, without distinction of class or of religion. The most prompt and energetic means for remedying the abuses in collecting the taxes, and especially the tithes, shall be considered. The system of direct collection shall gradually, and as soon as possible, be substituted for the plan of farming, in all the branches of the revenues of the State. As long as the present system remains in force, all agents of the Government and all members of the Medjlis shall be forbidden, under the severest penalties, to become lessees of any farming contracts which are announced for public competition, or to have any beneficial interest in carrying them out. The local taxes shall, as far as possible, be so imposed as not to affect the sources of production, or to hinder the progress of internal commerce.'

Now, it is important to bear in mind the fact which, indeed, the Sultan himself states, apparently without any feeling of shame; that the promises made in this Hatt-i-Sherif of 1856, were only the reiteration of those made in the Hatt-i-Humaïoun of 1839, and these again were only the reiteration of promises made in the older Tanzimat, and that this reiteration was made necessary by the fact that the promises made in the first instance, and re-promised in the second, were still unfulfilled. Now let us ask what has been the fate of this third instrument, with its reiteration of the unfulfilled engagements of the two preceding documents? Have these promises been better kept than the self-same promises made thirty years ago?

The Hatt-i-Sherif has never been even promulgated. It is unknown throughout the whole of Turkey. Not one promise has been performed, not one stipulation has been fulfilled, and yet in the face of these facts, even members of Parliament, officers of the Government, presuming upon the almost universal ignorance which prevails respecting that country, venture to speak in the House of Commons of the fidelity of Turkey to her engagements!

By the Tanzimat, the Hatt-i-Humaïoun of 1839, and Hatt-i-Sherif of 1856, three editions of the same unfulfilled promises, it was declared, as we have seen, amongst other things, that Christians might hold landed property in all parts of the empire as freely as Mussulmans, and also that there should be perfect equality as to taxation between the Mussulmans and non-Mussulmans of Turkey.

What attempt has been made to carry out these simple requirements of justice?

Amongst the questions issued by Sir Henry Bulwer to the English consuls in Turkey, occurs the following:—'4. Can Christians hold landed property on equal condition with Turks? and if not, where is the difference?'

To this question Mr Calvert of Salonica replies—'As regards the acquisition of landed property, a Christian is not allowed to purchase any belonging to a Turk.'*

* Report of Consuls on the Condition of Christians in Turkey, p. 10.

Since, then, nearly every acre of land at the present moment belongs to the Turks, the refusal to allow Christians to purchase such lands amounts almost to a prohibition of their purchasing any land. Again, on this subject Mr Finn of Jerusalem reports— 'Native Christians are precisely on equal terms with Mussulmans in regard to the tenure of landed property, though in acquiring it they are exposed to pecuniary and other annoyances to which a Moslem would not be exposed.' *

Mr Skene of Aleppo thus answers Sir Henry Bulwer's question :—' Freehold property, the best of tenures, is within the reach of the Sultan's Christian subjects. The fear, however, of unfair treatment deters them from becoming landholders.' †

To the same effect Acting-Consul Zohrab says— 'Christians are now permitted to possess real property, but the obstacles which they meet with when they attempt to acquire it are so many and vexatious that very few have as yet dared to brave them.' ‡

What those obstacles are which prevent Christians from acquiring and holding land he proceeds to state in these words :—' Christians are permitted by

---

* Report of Consuls on the Condition of Christians in Turkey, p. 27.
† Ibid. p. 50. ‡ Ibid. p. 54.

law to possess landed property, but the difficulties opposed to their acquiring are so great that few have as yet dared to face them. As far as the mere purchase goes, no difficulties are made—a Christian can buy and take possession; it is when he has got his land into order, or when the Mussulman who has sold has overcome the pecuniary difficulties which compelled him to sell, that the Christian feels the helplessness of his position and the insincerity of the Government. Steps are then taken by the original proprietor, or some relative of his, to reclaim the land from the Christian, generally on one of the following pleas: that the original owner, not being sole proprietor, had no right to sell; that the ground being "meraah," or grazing-ground, could not be sold; that the deeds of transfer being defective the sale had not been legally made. Under one or other of these pleas the Christian is in nineteen cases out of twenty dispossessed, and he may then deem himself fortunate if he gets back the price he gave. Few, a very few, have been able to obtain justice; but I must say that the majority of these owe their good fortune not to the justice of their cause, but to the influence of some powerful Mussulman.' *

* Report of Consuls on the Condition of Christians in Turkey, p. 55.

This, then, is the way in which this stipulation is carried out in Turkey. Christians may hold land, but—they must not purchase any belonging to a Turk. As at present scarcely any land belongs to any one else than a Turk, this is virtually to prevent all such purchases. But beyond this the dangers which threaten those who attempt to do that which the law declares they may do are so real, that few are hardy enough to brave them, and when they do, having paid the price for their possession, no sooner is the land brought under cultivation, than the original owner is at liberty to reclaim it, and having dragged the unfortunate purchaser into a court of law where his evidence cannot be received, he may re-enter his old possession with impunity, for even documentary evidence made in favour of a Christian is rejected by these courts of injustice.

(3) Nor has the stipulation of equality of taxation been any more regarded than that which declared the right of the Christian to hold land. One provision of the Tanzimat was, that arbitrary taxation of the Christian peasant was to cease. This has never been fulfilled, except in a way which the petitioners could scarcely have contemplated.

On this head we have the following observations in Mr Calvert's report :—'The Turkish Government has too long neglected the interests of the two classes of the population upon whose well-being the prosperity of the country mainly depends, namely, the agricultural and mercantile classes. Almost every other consideration ought to have been sacrificed for the promotion of their interests. Like the Turkish landed proprietors, the State appears to care not how its revenues are raised, provided it receives them.'

* * * * * *

'We have an instance of this in the manner in which the direct taxes were assessed upon the Christians on the promulgation of the "Tanzimati Hairiyé," which was intended to put a stop to the then existing systems of exactions. The Rayah population, on being called upon, promptly furnished statements of the exact amount of the contributions they had been arbitrarily subjected to in addition to the lawful taxes; and since it was presumed that they had been able to satisfy all the requisitions made upon them, the Government, I am told, forthwith assessed them with the whole amount, which they pay at the present moment.' *

* * * * * *

* Report of Consuls on Condition of Christians in Turkey, pp. 8, 9.

'As the Mussulman peasantry are not as well off as they might be, the distinction between the condition of the Christians and that of the Mussulmans in the villages is in some respects only relative. One point of difference consists in the fact that the irregularities of the tax and tithes collectors, and the excesses of the police force, not to speak of the depredations of brigands, are practised to a larger extent and with more barefacedness on the Christian than on the Mussulman peasantry. It is, however, extremely difficult to define the extent of the difference, and quite impossible to prove the facts on which the general statement of its existence is founded. But I feel persuaded that, without admitting any special claim of the Christians on our sympathy, the tacit submission of the Christians to the abuses in question, and to others of a harassing character, has conduced to their perpetuation at the hands of the notoriously rapacious tax and tithes farmers. The Mussulman peasantry are not so extensively imposed upon, because the superior chance which their complaints have of being listened to by a District Government in which the element of their co-religionists preponderates, causes them to be regarded with greater respect. The Mussulman peasantry, nevertheless, suffer from the same causes as their fellow-labourers on the soil, only to a smaller degree. There is, however, a positive difference, and a very important one, in the condition of the Christian peasants in the farms ("tchiftliks") held by Turkish proprietors. They are forcibly tied to the spot by means of a perpetual and even hereditary debt which their landlord contrives to fasten upon them. This has practically reduced many of the peasant families to a state of serfdom. As an illustration, I may mention, that when a tchiftlik is sold, the bonds of the peasantry are transferred with the stock to the new proprietor. In Thessaly there are Christians who own farms on the same conditions. Upon one occasion, in which the landlord, who was a merchant, had become a bankrupt, I remember noticing, that amongst the assets borne on his balance-sheet there figured the aggregate amount of the peasants' debts to him, and it formed a rather large item.' *

These oppressions and exactions, according to the testimony of Mr Skene, so far from diminishing, have greatly increased of late years. It is significant of the utterly hopeless condition of the Turkish Government, that even administrative re-

* Report of Consuls on Condition of Christians in Turkey, pp. 10, 11.

form becomes a fresh engine of evil to the overburdened Christian. It has been the practice of late years to send an assistant or kehaya with the Pasha—a kind of deputy Pasha, to check and report the actions of that officer, with what effect Mr Skene will tell us. 'In my humble opinion, the experiment of municipal institutions was made in a manner not in harmony with the existing state of the country. The feudal system of the East had degenerated when it produced the great barons of Turkey in the first quarter of the present century, Ali Tepedeleni, Ali of Stolatz, Kara Osman Oglu, Chassan Oglu, Haznadar Oglu, and others, equally powerful and independent, and it had reduced the body of the people to actual servitude. The spirit of industry was crushed by the narrow maxims of a military aristocracy. The country was on the verge of ruin. A counterpoise was sought for the oppression of Pashas of the old school. The remedy has oûtweighed the evil, and instead of one tyrant there are now many tyrants, each grasping his own advantage, and all inferior to the Pasha in qualifications for government. The desired control exists, but the local magnates are unworthy of the trust. The power of the functionaries sent from Constantinople, which is a whole century in advance of the provinces, is paralyzed by the corrupt action of the Ayans. A good Pasha is hampered; a bad one not checked. Men of integrity and public spirit may come from the capital, but are not to be found in the towns of the interior. The Pasha of the present day is an improvement on the old feudal Satrap; the unchanging Ayan is still a man of the same stamp; and the better is thus controlled by the worse. Composed of cruel, venal, and rapacious accomplices, the Medjlis oppresses the people and enriches itself, while Pashas are powerless, when willing, to cope with its collusive chicanery. Possessed of superior local information and experience, wielding a dangerous influence over the lower orders, which fear their iron rule, and well versed in all the trickery of Oriental intrigue, they rarely fail soon to reduce the most zealous Pasha to the condition of a mere instrument in their hands. . . . I have followed the same familiar phases of provincial government with unvarying issue in Bosnia, Bulgaria, and Roumelia, in Asia Minor and Syria, and I have thus been forced into strong convictions on the subject, which I hope to be held excused for thus expressing freely.'*

* Report of Consuls on Condition of Christians in Turkey, pp. 51, 52.

Mr Abbot, of Monastir, adds his testimony to the same effect. 'In giving my humble opinion on this subject, I am far from taking the part of the Turks, and exonerating the conduct of some of the Turkish officials. Abuses, and to a great extent, exist in this Province as well as in others, and the evils caused by these abuses are of such a nature as to admit of remedy.

'For instance, a Pasha is apparently an honest man, but his Kehaya or Intendant is venal, and then the inhabitants have to suffer from the rapacity of a man whose advice has so much deliberative power with the Pasha, who, perhaps indolent and weak, allows himself to be influenced by an unprincipled man in whom he has entire confidence.

'Then come next the Beys, who sit in the Medjlises. Natives of the place where they hold their office, and with great local interests to protect, they connive, for a trifle, at illegal acts, if, by doing so, their interests are in any way promoted, and hence affix their seals to decisions which have not the slightest particle of justice.'*

The same testimony, again, is borne by Mr Zohrab as to the hopelessness of expecting any real

* Report of Consuls on Condition of Christians in Turkey, p. 4.

amelioration of the condition of the Christians from the hands of the officers of the Sultan. Speaking of the Christians he says:—'In the belief that the direct administration of the Porte would materially ameliorate their position, they were induced, in 1850, to lend a hearty assistance to Omer Pasha, and to their aid must be attributed the rapid success of the Turkish arms. Their hopes were disap-. pointed. That they were benefited by the change there can be no doubt, but the extent did not nearly come up to their expectation. They saw, with delight, the extinction of the Spahi privileges and of the *corvée*, but the imposition of new and heavy taxes, the gross peculation of the *employés* sent from Constantinople, and the demands of the army filled them with disappointments and dismay; and, with these causes for complaint, their previous servile condition was almost forgotten. Their hopes had been raised high to be cruelly disappointed; their pecuniary position was aggravated, while their social position was but slightly improved.'

* * * * * *

'Oppression cannot now be carried on as openly as formerly, but it must not be supposed that, because the Government *employés* do not generally appear as the oppressors, the Christians are well treated and protected. A certain impunity, for which the Government must be rendered responsible, is allowed to the Mussulmans. This impunity, while it does not extend to permitting the Christians to be treated as they formerly were treated, is so far unbearable and unjust, in that it permits the Mussulmans to despoil them with heavy exactions. False imprisonments are of daily occurrence. A Christian has but a small chance of exculpating himself when his opponent is a Mussulman.

* * * * * *

'Such being, generally speaking, the course pursued by the Government towards the Christians in the capital of the province where the Consular Agents of the different Powers reside and can exercise some degree of control, it may easily be guessed to what extent the Christians, in the remoter districts, suffer who are governed by Mudirs generally fanatical and unacquainted with the law.'*

So uniform is the course of injustice practised towards the Christians, that the words of a consul at one end of the empire seems but an echo of those already spoken by another at the opposite extremity. Mr Abbot, consul at the Dardanelles, says:—'It

* Report of Consuls on Condition of Christians in Turkey, p. 54.

might reasonably have been expected that the general condition of the country ought, by this time, to have so far improved as to have inspired the whole population with the certain conviction that any just claim, even from the humblest individual, would meet with a fair investigation; that the Porte would have devised such checks over its functionaries as to prevent the possibility of the powers confided to them being abused, and would have exercised the utmost vigilance over their conduct. Such, unfortunately, is not the case. Too much power is confided to the chief local authorities; the laws and regulations are framed so carelessly—their construction is so defective (no provision being made for securing adhesion to them)—that it is obvious they are the work of persons inexperienced in the art of legislation. The consequence is, that with a host of officials who suffer no opportunity to escape them of abusing their power whenever they can derive any substantial advantage therefrom, the laws are either eluded or converted into instruments of oppression.

* * * * * *

'I trace, as one of the principal causes which renders the laws, framed in a most laudable spirit, perfectly inoperative, the fact of the Government trusting the welfare of the province to the sole goodwill of the Governors, believing that they will carry out implicitly its instructions, without requiring proof of their being fulfilled. Thus, for instance, in the Porte's Proclamation of the 2nd of March, 1846, the Governors and other authorities are expressly forbidden to receive bribes, to impose " corvées " without payment, &c.; but I observe that the only check attempted to be imposed is, strange to say, confided to the Governors themselves, who are commanded to report any person infringing this order. The Porte appears to have forgotten that the Governor himself might be the first person to set this order at defiance; so that it is rendered nugatory to all intents and purposes.' *

Amongst other evils which press exclusively upon the Christians, Major Cox, writing from Bucharest, but speaking of the state of the whole province of Bulgaria, says :—' The Christians are exposed to the necessity of entertaining strangers, and the others are not.

'The Christians are the subjects of "hanghariyeh" or forced labour, and the others are not.

'The Christians are frequently obliged to give

* Report of Consuls on Condition of Christians in Turkey, p. 76.

their labour to the Mussulmans of the village at a low rate of wages.' *

The oppressive way in which the Government exacts the tithe of all agricultural produce, is made to press most injuriously upon the Christians.

'The crops, after being cut, are sometimes two months on the ground before the tithe-farmer comes, and until then the people dare not remove them; their value is of course much diminished by the ravages of the animals and of the weather. If this tithe-tax could be assessed it would be a great boon, and the whole of the taxes collected in money after the harvest.

'It is stated that in many instances the cost to the villagers of entertaining the collectors of the "iltizam" has nearly doubled that tax.' †

But I will not fatigue the reader by travelling through this wearying record of oppression. Holding his life, the honour of his family, and his property at the mercy of his Mussulman neighbour, who hates him on account of his religion, and envies the results of his industry; weighed down by Government taxation, and oppressed beyond even that by the rapacity

* Report of Consuls on Condition of Christians in Turkey, p. 58.
† Ibid. p. 60.

of the farmers of taxes; without help from the tribunals, where his evidence cannot be heard; mocked by promises of protection by the Sultan which have never been fulfilled—the lot of the Christian peasant, the condition of those who numerically are more than three-fourths of the people of European Turkey, and a very large proportion of the population of Asia Minor and Syria, is one of despair. He sees around him the bitter tokens of increasing wrong. His hard and cruel bondage has not sufficed to extinguish the love of home and the desire for children, and a blessing has gone with him; so that whilst his stern taskmasters are diminishing, he sees his own race increasing, and is doomed to feel the intolerable sufferings which are instigated by the jealousy excited in the breast of the Mussulmans by the impression, which is gaining force every day, that they are retrograding to the advantage of the Christian. Indeed—'This feeling has acquired such influence in the subordinate Medjlises, that when any case of oppression takes place on the part of the populace, courts are disposed to assist in it.' *

Shut out as the subject race is from the acquisition of land, their attention has been turned chiefly

* Report of Consuls on Condition of Christians in Turkey, p. 36.

TURKISH PROMISES AND NON-PERFORMANCES. 161

to trade, and almost the whole of this throughout Turkey has passed into their hands, and as a consequence we read, in the report of another consul, that—'The progress of the Christians has reached a degree which is becoming dangerous to them: the Mussulmans are jealous of their prosperity in trade.' *

(4) Another concession, in favour of the Christians of Turkey, which the Western Powers of Europe required from the Sultan was, that the armies of that country should be recruited alike from the Mussulman and non-Mussulman portions of the population. It was felt that so long as the Christians were forbidden to be armed, whilst the rest of the subjects of Turkey were allowed the use of arms, and whilst the soldiery of the empire was exclusively drawn from one race, those classes of the people which were excluded from the army and not allowed to be armed were exposed to a certain disadvantage, and that their defenceless condition invited attack. Both in the Hatt-i-Sherif of 1839, and again in the Hatt-i-Humaïoun of 1856, it was promised that this distinction should be abolished, and that the army should be drawn from the population of Turkey without distinction of creed.

* Report of Consuls on Condition of Christians in Turkey, p. 50.

It may be well to cite the express words of the Hatt-i-Humaïoun of 1856. In the eighth clause of this document the Sultan declared that from henceforth 'All the subjects of my empire, without distinction, shall be received into the military and civil schools of the State.' In the fifteenth clause he promised that 'there shall be published, with as little delay as possible, a law with full provisions as to the manner of admission into, and of the duties of my Christian and other non-Mussulman subjects while in, the army.' It was promised, and here the matter has rested. No Christian is allowed to bear arms; the army is exclusively Mussulman. But not only is this pledge given to the Western Powers deliberately violated, the pledge extorted, though unfulfilled, has been turned into a fresh engine of oppression. Christians are not only excluded—they are subject to an oppressive tax on the ground that they are so excluded.

The tenth of Sir Henry Bulwer's questions is as follows:—'10. Would the Christian population like to enter the military service instead of paying the tax which procures them exemption; and which would they gain most by—serving in the army, or paying the said tax?'*

* Report of Consuls on Condition of Christians in Turkey, p. 3.

TURKISH PROMISES AND NON-PERFORMANCES. 163

To this Mr Abbot, of Monastir, replies:—'Christians would prefer entering the army instead of paying the exemption tax, provided they were formed into separate regiments, and were held out the prospect of advancing as much as Mussulmans would in similar positions. If this were the case, they would gain most by serving in the army.' *

Mr Finn, of Jerusalem, answers this question in these words:—'Excepting in Jerusalem, where they are too much priest-ridden, the Christians do wish to serve personally in the army instead of paying the substitution tax, and consider that they and their people would gain by it in consideration. I am told that, in several parts of Syria, the youthful Christian population have petitioned for the privilege of serving personally in the army, even without requiring to be placed in separate companies or regiments.' †

Again, Mr J. E. Blunt, of Pristina:—'It is the impression of the Undersigned that the Christians, the peasantry, which forms the bulk of their population, would prefer to enter the military service than pay the commutation-tax. . . . The Christians

* Report of Consuls on Condition of Christians in Turkey, p. 5.
† Ibid. p. 28.

would gain more by serving in the army than by paying the tax.' *

Mr Moore, consul at Beyrout, says:—'I think they would prefer entering the army to paying the tax, if there could be enrolled purely Christian regiments, officered by Christians; but they much prefer paying the tax to serving in the army with the condition of being drafted into Turkish regiments with Turkish officers. They would gain most, I conceive, by entering the army under the former arrangement than by paying the tax.' † How the clauses of the Hatt-i-Humaïoun of 1856 have been fulfilled we may learn from the latest blue book on Turkey. Sir Henry Elliot, writing on June 8th of the present year to Lord Derby, says, 'The necessity of putting an end to the distinction which has been maintained between the two religions has long been admitted in principle, and while one clause of the Hatt-i-Humaïoun of 1856, drawn up under the advice of the Western Powers, stated that Christians should be admitted to the military schools, another declared that measures should be immediately concerted for admitting them into the army,' and he

* Report of Consuls on Condition of Christians in Turkey, p. 36.
† Ibid. p. 71.

adds the significant comment—'*These two clauses have hitherto remained a dead letter.*' *

A difference of opinion exists as to whether the Christians of Turkey, on the whole, would or would not be better off by paying the heavy exemption-tax, or by serving in the army; but no difference of opinion is possible as to the fraud practised upon the Western Powers by the non-fulfilment of the promise made by the Porte. It is pleaded by some of the consuls that, under the present condition of the Christians, and in face of the injustice practised towards them, it would be dangerous for the Sultan to put arms into their hands. But this is only an additional reason why the contracting Powers should insist upon this stipulation being faithfully carried out. Compel the Government of Turkey to fulfil its obligation in this respect, and that Government will be compelled, as a necessary antecedent, to ameliorate the condition of the Christians. At present the Christians are not armed, because they are so unjustly used, that it would be dangerous to place arms in their hands. By insisting upon this stipulation being fulfilled, we insist then upon their being fairly treated.

* Correspondence respecting the Affairs of Turkey, No. 3, 1876, p. 267.

It is absurd to suppose that a nation of more than twenty-four millions of persons should require the constant wet-nursing of England to carry them safely through their second infancy. Twenty-four millions of free men might defend themselves against the world in arms. The defensive strength of such a nation is far greater than the offensive power of Russia. It is because the strength of the Mussulman is exhausted in watching against and in oppressing the non-Mussulman portion of the empire that there exists any necessity of aid from England. If we compel Turkey to do justice to all her subjects, we shall obviate the necessity for English blood being wasted and English treasure consumed in defence of such a Power. Tell Turkey that she must henceforth rely upon her own subjects, and she will be forced to adopt a generous policy towards them. We are bearing at this moment the additional weight of seventy millions to our National Debt: we have to deplore the death of many thousands of Englishmen in the Crimean campaign: we maintain, at a great expense, a large Mediterranean fleet to be ready to defend Turkey against all assailants—only because the Sultan will not do justice to his Christian subjects. Had he done so, there would have been no Russian War; and had the Czar been ever so ambitious, ever so warlike, Turkey, but for this standing wrong against the great bulk of her people, might, without aid from England, France, and Italy, have resisted all the assaults of the legions of the Northern autocrat. Whilst we are willing to pay for the injustice of Turkey towards her own subjects, we encourage her to persist in that injustice.

(5) But there is another subject about which Sir Henry Bulwer professes incredulity, and on which he requires information, and that is the enforced conversions from Christianity — the compulsory adoption of the Mahomedan creed, in order to escape persecution and death. Nothing can show either the utter ignorance of Sir Henry Bulwer as to the state of Turkey or the unfairness of his questions than that he should ask for information on the subject. He knew at the time of sending out the list of questions that in the massacres of the Lebanon and Damascus whole villages, hundreds of men, women, and children, had been compelled to adopt the Mahomedan faith in order to escape death in its most appalling forms. Sir Henry Bulwer knew, on the evidence of Lord Dufferin and of Mr Cyril Graham, that thousands of those who then perished died martyrs for Christianity. That the alternative of death, or accepting the Mahomedan creed, was

presented not only to men, but to women, and even to girls of tender age, and that thousands deliberately preferred the cruellest martyrdoms to abandoning their religion. When we talk of the imperfect faith of our brethren in the East—when we are told of their low morality, be this remembered to their everlasting honour, that in the middle of the nineteenth century between five and six thousand, at the least, on that occasion, accepted death rather than deny their belief in Christ!

(6) But a survey of the condition of the Christians in Turkey would be incomplete if I were to pass over all consideration of their moral state. The advocates of the Government of that country—the apologists for the rule of the Sultan—tell us that the Christians—the large mass of the people of Turkey —have 'exaggerated notions of nationality and political freedom;'* that they have 'no independence of character;'† that they are 'ignorant;' 'miserly at home, abject without support, and insolent where unduly protected;'‡ that they are 'lying, intriguing;'§ and that their clergy and

---

* Report of Consuls on Condition of Christians in Turkey, p. 8.
† Ibid. p. 20.   ‡ Ibid. p. 49.   § Ibid. p. 64.

municipal officers are 'rapacious,' and that the whole race is 'degraded and pusillanimous.' *

I have no doubt but that much of this is true. It is the curse of slavery that it brings forth in men the fruits of slavery; and when we see such fruit, we are sure what the root must be. I know no heavier accusation against the Government of Turkey than that it makes men abject and lying, pusillanimous and miserly; that it destroys independence of character, and that it degrades the whole man. The peasant, whose life and the lives of his children are at the mercy of his neighbours, cringes and submits to degrading acts until he acquires the habit of cringing. The man whose property may be seized at any moment by the meanest village official will, I am afraid, pretty generally 'intrigue' and 'lie' to preserve his hard-earned and dearly-prized possessions. This is the aspect which human nature invariably presents. But is this any excuse for slavery and oppression? Surely it is but its severest reproach. If the Christians of Turkey were invariably honest, munificent, manly—if, in short, they had all the virtues of free men, then I for one should be content that they should abide under the

* Mr Layard, in House of Commons, May 29, 1863. .

rule of the Sultan. The assertion that these virtues are not to be found—at least, in profusion—but that the subject races are degraded by vices of this kind, is the strongest condemnation which can be uttered against that system of government by which they are weighed down and debased. Slaves are not freemen, neither have they the virtues of freedom. This is why slavery is so bitter a wrong, not that it diminishes the pleasures of the senses, but that it destroys the dignity of manhood; and because I long for the day when our brethren of the East may be distinguished for independence of character — when they may be truthful, honest, courageous—in a word, free men, I desire they may be free. They cannot possess these qualities of the heart and soul so long as they are trampled under-foot by their present masters. It is because you cannot graft these virtues upon the stock of abject subjection, that we ought to strive for their deliverance from their present hard bondage.

> 'That man's half-virtue Jove takes quite away,
> That once is sun-burnt with the servile day.' *

It is because you cannot gather grapes from thorns, nor figs from thistles, that the thorns and the thistles should no longer be permitted to hinder

* Chapman: Odyssey xvii.

the growth of those fruits which they cannot themselves produce.

But we overlook much of the evils of slavery when we only consider its effects upon the bodies and souls of the enslaved race. It spreads beyond these: it debases and corrupts the master oftentimes more than the slave. This—according to the testimony of all travellers, of all who know anything of the condition of Turkey—is the result of slavery in that country. The subject races are 'degraded and pusillanimous,' so much so indeed that, in many places, they have lost heart, and have become meekly submissive to injustice;* but the ruling caste—the masters of these slaves—have sunk to lower depths than these, so that, degraded as the Christians are, and degraded because oppressed, yet in them alone lies the hope that the people of the countries stretching from the Black Sea to Aden will ever again lift up their heads and be numbered amongst the nations.

On this matter I prefer to pursue the same course which I have already followed, and to allow others to speak rather than, by generalizing their testimony, to weaken its force.

* Report of Consuls on Condition of Christians in Turkey, p. 65.

In Mr Senior's diary this conversation is recorded:—' Soon after I left C. D., E. F. called on us.

' " What impression," he said, " does the East produce on you ? "

' " The East," I said, " is not quite new to me, as I have passed some months in Egypt."

' " Egypt," he answered, " is not a fair specimen. The government of Egypt is as superior to the Mahomedan government as the docile laborious Fellah is to the brutal Turk."

' " I have had time," I said, " only to look at the exterior. I see a capital, the streets of which are impassable to wheels, and scarcely to be traversed on foot; I see a country without a road; I see a palace of the Sultan's on every promontory of the Bosporus; I see vast tracts of unoccupied land, and more dogs than human beings; these appearances are not favourable to the government or to the people."

' " If you have the misfortune," he answered, " as I have had, to live among Turks for between two and three years, your opinions will be still less favourable. In government and in religion Turkey is a detritus. All that gave her strength, all that gave her consistency, has gone, what remains is crumbling into powder. The worst parts of her detestable religion, hatred of improvement, and hatred of the unbeliever; the worst parts of her detestable government, violence, extortion, treachery, and fraud, are all that she has retained. Never was there a country that more required to be conquered. Our support merely delays her submission to that violent remedy." ' *

Again, in the same volume :—' The Turks of Europe are not producers ; they are a parasitical population, which lives only by plundering the Christians. Let this be made impossible, or even difficult, and they will emigrate or die out. The Turkish power in Bulgaria and Roumelia might thus fall of itself without conquest, as it has already done virtually in Servia, and in the Principalities.' †

And a little further on :—' " Turkey," said W., " exists for two purposes. First, to act as a dog in the manger, and to prevent any Christian power from possessing a country which she herself in her present state is unable to govern or to protect. And, secondly, for the benefit of some fifty or sixty bankers and usurers, and some thirty or forty pashas, who make fortunes out of its spoils. It is the land of jobs. All these palaces, all these terraced gardens, are the fruit of jobs, when they are not the fruit of some-

* Senior, pp. 27, 28. † Ibid. p. 32.

thing worse. All the most respectable statesmen are jobbers. Reschid Pasha during his different vizierships sold to himself at low prices large tracts of public land. He built a palace at Balti Liman, and sold it for £200,000 to the Sultan, who made a present of it to his daughter married to Reschid's son."' *

Another conversation is reported in these words: —'We talked of the degeneracy of the Turks. "How do you account," I asked, "for the strange fact, if it be a fact, that in proportion as they have improved their institutions, in proportion as life and property have been more secure, their wealth and their numbers have diminished? How comes it that the improvement which gives prosperity to every other nation ruins them?"'

'"It *is* a fact," said Y., "that while their institutions have improved, their wealth and population have diminished. Many causes have contributed to this deterioration. The first and great one is, that they are not producers. They have neither diligence, intelligence, nor forethought. No Turk is an improving landlord, or even a repairing landlord. When he has money, he spends it on objects of immediate gratification. His most permanent in-

* Senior, p. 84.

vestment is a timber palace, to last about as long as its builder. His only professions are shop-keeping and service. He cannot engage in any foreign commerce, as he speaks no language but his own. No one ever heard of a Turkish house of business, or of a Turkish banker, or merchant, or manufacturer. If he has lands or houses, he lives on their rent; if he has money, he spends it, or employs it in stocking a shop, in which he can smoke and gossip all day long. The only considerable enterprise in which he ever engages is the farming some branch of the public revenue." ' *

But, not to multiply extracts, to testify to a fact which is illustrated in almost every page of this valuable volume, I will only add the following :—' " The distinguishing characteristic of the real Asiatic is, intellectual sterility and unfitness for change. One nation, to save itself trouble, declares that its laws shall be-immutable. Another institutes caste, and makes all further improvement impossible. Another protects itself against new ideas, by refusing all intercourse with foreigners. An Asiatic had rather copy than try to invent, rather acquiesce than discuss, rather attribute events to destiny than to causes that can be inquired into and explained.

* Senior, pp. 210, 211.

His only diplomacy is war; his only internal means of government are poison, the stick, and the bowstring.

'"In the Turk these peculiarities are exaggerated. Whatever be his purpose, he uses the means which require the least thought. If he has to create a local government, he simply hands over to the Pasha all the powers of the Sultan. If he wants money, he takes it wherever he can find it; and if he cannot get it by force, he puts up to auction power, justice, the prosperity, and indeed the subsistence, of his subjects. He averts the dangers of a disputed succession by killing all the nephews of the Sultan, or preventing any from coming into existence. He relies on the rain for washing his streets, on the dogs for keeping them free from offal, on the sun for making passable the tracks which he calls roads, and on the climate for enabling him to live in his timber house without repairing it. For everything else he relies on Allah, and entreats God to do for him what he is too torpid to do for himself. His fatalism is, in fact, indolence in its most exaggerated form. It is an escape, not only from exertion, but from deliberation.

'" Our attempts to improve the Turks put me in mind of the old story of the people who tried to wash the negro white. He never was, or will be, or can be anything but a barbarian." ' *

Lord Hobart and Mr Forster, in their report on the state of Turkish finance, speak of Turkey as possessing—' An army scarcely sufficient to ensure the defence of the frontier from marauding tribes, and powerless in the face of a fanatical outbreak; with a police, which in many parts of the empire casts not even a shadow of restraint upon the thriving trading of brigandage, and with production and commerce paralyzed for want of roads.' †

But, on this subject, it is possible to cite Sir Henry Bulwer himself as a witness, the more valuable, because his Turkish predilections are sufficiently notorious not to permit of our believing that he would exaggerate the evils of this empire of anarchy. Speaking of Syria, he says :—' To expect the same state of things in Syria that exists in a well-, or even ill-, governed province in Europe, is out of the question. The warlike and more than half-barbarous mountaineers are in one quarter habituated to a state of military independence. In another, the wild Arabs of the Desert have through all times defied

* Senior, pp. 227, 228.
† Report on the Financial Condition of Turkey, Dec. 1861, p. 32.

civilization, and resorted to plunder wherever there was not a superior force to overawe their temerity, or punish their misdeeds. In the plains there exists a peasantry thrifty and industrious, but for ages oppressed and subdued. How can all these, by the wand of an enchanter, be at once called into a homogeneous class of cultivators, artizans, shopkeepers, and merchants obedient to the law, and acknowledging that equality before it which distinguishes the citizens of our modern communities? It appears that, for some time at least, there is only a choice between the two extremes of disorder generated by licence, and submission, the consequence of power, which will rarely be unaccompanied by oppression. At the present time, however, these two extremes appear unhappily associated. Wherever the Turk is sufficiently predominant to be implicitly obeyed, laziness, corruption, extravagance, and penury mark his rule; and wherever he is too feeble to exert more than a doubtful and nominal authority, the system of government which prevails is that of the Arab robber and the lawless Highland chieftain.' *

And yet, according to the testimony of Mr Brant, quoted at page 50, it is evident that the task of

* Papers on Administrative and Financial Reform in Turkey, 1858—1861, pp. 32, 33.

TURKISH PROMISES AND NON-PERFORMANCES. 179

reducing Syria to order is only hopeless, because it is under the government of Turks.

In answer to Sir Henry Bulwer's question to the consuls—'What measures do you think could best be taken to improve generally the condition of the country?'*

Mr Charles Blunt, of Smyrna, replies:—'Previously to suggesting any measures, it is most undoubtedly, under existing circumstances, a question of very serious import whether, by attempting a reorganization, and consequently disturbing the present state of things, any beneficial results could be obtained. My foregoing replies have shown that, when human life and property were secure, the state of the Christian races began to improve simultaneously, it may be said, with agriculture and commerce. The more than richness of the soil, and well-known superior intelligence of the Christian over the Mahometan races, mainly contributed to that improvement; therefore the now daily-increasing means of instruction, so largely availed of by the Christians, but unheeded by the Turks; the facility of communication with more civilized nations by steam, and the introduction of railways, will probably do more for

* Report of Consuls on Condition of Christians in Turkey, p. 4.

the general good of the country, even under the present faulty system, than the introduction of new measures which the Turks cannot or will not understand, and I may add, have neither the desire nor capacity for carrying out.

'In making the latter remarks, however strong they may appear, I shall venture to add, for my justification, that, with a people with whom the idea of patriotism is wanting; people in whose characters apathy and procrastination are predominant; people whose ideas are, in the extreme sense of the words, selfish and sensual; people whose existing social and moral evils add to the daily-increasing degradation of the country; with such sorry elements to work with, the introduction of new measures might probably tend to disturb the present steadily-progressing intelligence and prosperity of the country.' *

Nor is there any hope of improvement in the way of education:—'The ignorance of the Mussulmans on all educational matters is notorious: indeed, they delude themselves with the idea that they are so infinitely superior to the conquered races that it would be derogatory in them to improve their minds in the same way as the Christians do. The Rayahs have

* Report of Consuls on Condition of Christians in Turkey, p. 34

begun of late years to understand the immense importance of education, and the great advantages to be derived from it, and they demonstrate a most praiseworthy desire for acquiring knowledge and for having their children properly educated.

'The utmost that a Turk will attempt is to follow the old beaten track of his ancestors, in merely learning to read the Koran, and to write sufficiently well to be able to compose a letter with tolerable correctness and elegance. The Turkish Khoja, or schoolmaster, is totally ignorant of geography, general history, natural science, and modern languages; indeed, the Turks deem such knowledge to be quite useless.' *

No wonder that every one who has seen the country, has lived in Turkish society, and is able to observe, is in despair of preserving this empire as at present constituted : — ' "As for the integrity of Turkey," said W., "as a permanent arrangement, it is impossible. We may dose her with Hatt-i-Humaïouns, but she is past physic, 'nullum remedium agit in cadaver.' She is worse than a corpse; she is a corpse in a state of decomposition." ' †

'This country is a *pourriture*. To civilize the

* Report of Consuls on Condition of Christians in Turkey, p. 87.   † Senior, p. 86.

Mussulman is impossible. All that we can do is to try to raise the Christian. He has borne on his shoulders far too long this *cadavre*.' *

If there exists any gleam of hope, however faint, for this Turkish race, it is in the overthrow of the Government of the country; for ignorant, and inert, and sensual as the whole people may be, the governing body, the officials throughout the empire, are more depraved even than the Mussulmans whom they govern, and under the firm and equitable rule of a Christian people it might even be possible to save the poorer classes amongst the Turks from that utter extinction which surely awaits them if the Government of the Sultan continue much longer:—

'Mr Blunt was for twenty years consul at Salonica. I asked him which population he preferred, the Salonicans or the Smyrniotes.

' "There is not much," he said, "to choose between them. The poorer, the humbler the Turk is, the better he is; as he mixes with the world, and as he gets money and power, he deteriorates. In the lowest class I have sometimes found truth, honesty, and gratitude; in the middle classes, seldom; in the highest, never. Even the lowest classes are changed for the worse. Five and twenty years ago you could

* Senior, p. 147.

trust a bag of money to a porter for short distances, to a courier for long ones; it was the practice. No one ventures to do so now. The race, however, is rapidly dying out." ' *

And, again:—' "The Turk of the 15th century," answered Y., "was a different person from the Turk of the 19th.

' "He was athletic and vigorous, he lived in exercise and in the open air. He was not the sedentary smoking sensualist that he is now: but I will not deny that even the degenerate Turk has some virtues. He is sober. All classes are sober in eating, the great majority are sober in drinking. He is sober in conduct, he is not easily ruffled or easily excited. He is calm in both good and bad fortune. He is eminently hospitable and charitable. Unhappily his virtues wither under the rays of prosperity. The poor Turk is honest and humane, the Turkish private soldier is brave. The rich Turk is always an oppressor." ' †

The testimony of Lord Carlisle is to much the same effect:—' Among the lower orders of the people there is considerable simplicity and loyalty of character, and a fair disposition to be obliging and friendly. Among those who emerge from the mass,

* Senior, pp. 189, 190. † Ibid. p. 226.

and have the opportunities of helping themselves to the good things of the world, the exceptions from thorough-paced corruption and extortion are most rare; and in the whole conduct of public business and routine of official life, under much apparent courtesy and undeviating good-breeding, a spirit of servility, detraction, and vindictiveness appears constantly at work. The bulk of the people is incredibly uninformed and ignorant.' *

With one other extract from another traveller I quit this branch of my subject:—'To do any good in this country, or to see it done, a man ought to live to a patriarchal age, and to see the Turks dispossessed of the sovereignty forthwith. There is a malediction of heaven and a self-destructiveness on their whole system. I know them well—I have now lived many years among them; there are admirable qualities in the *poor* Turks, but their Government is a compound of ignorance, blundering, vice — vice of the most atrocious kind—and weakness and rottenness. And whatever becomes a part of Government, or in any way connected with it, by the fact becomes corrupt. Take the honestest Turk you can find, and put him in office and power, and then tell me three months afterwards what he is! He must conform to the

* Diary in Turkish Waters, p. 182.

general system, or cease to be in office. One little wheel, however subordinate it may be, would derange the whole machine if its teeth did not fit.' *

The only hope, however, for this country rests in the Christian population. The superiority of the Rayah or Christian subjects of the Porte to the Mussulmans is so notorious, that no traveller in Turkey can pass it by unnoticed. They are at present rising elastic under the hand of the oppressor, so that the nature of the vices, with which they are justly charged, are, because clearly the result of servitude, grounds of hope and reasonable expectation that in their hands and under their government these fertile countries of Europe and Asia may again blossom as the rose and be studded by smiling villages.

Again to make use of Mr Senior's diary:—
'*Monday, November* 16*th*.—I showed Y. the journal which I have been keeping here.

' "All that you have reported of me," he said, " is correct. And I think that you have well collected the opinions that prevail in Smyrna respecting the Turks. But I should like to see more about the Greeks. They are destined to play—indeed they

* Turkey and its Destiny, by Charles McFarlane. Vol. II. pp. 84, 85.

play now—a more important part than the Turks. I admit that they have great faults; that they are false, intriguing, and servile; that they have, in short, many of the bad qualities which might be expected from four hundred years of oppression. The wonder is, that they are not worse. We find that even Englishmen are worse for twenty or thirty years of residence among us. But their diligence, their public spirit, their ambition, their thirst for knowledge, and their sagacity, are beyond all praise."'*

Again:—'The Turks are idle and improvident. The Greek labourers are not good, one of them does not do half the work of an Englishman; but he does three times the work of a Turk, and I pay him three times the wages.'†

Mr J. E. Blunt, British consul at Pristina, though, in his report, he points out that 'the Christian peasant labours under certain disadvantages from which the Turks, in comparison, suffer little or not at all,' yet tells us that 'A Christian village is in general better formed and cleaner, its yards more stocked, and its inhabitants better clothed, than the Turkish.' ‡

* Senior, pp. 223, 224. † Ibid. p. 164.
‡ Report of Consuls on Condition of Christians in Turkey, p. 35.

But, on this point, we hardly require the opinions of consuls, nor even the sad pictures which travellers give us of the contrast between the decaying Turkish village, or, more frequently, the clump of cypresses and the deserted cemetery, which alone show where a Turkish village has been, and the Christian hamlet embosomed in trees and tracked from afar by the sounds of joyous infancy. The one fact that, in every province of Turkey, the population is rapidly declining—that scarcely a town in the empire can be pointed out, in which whole quarters have not totally disappeared within the last few years, ' or have left nothing behind them but ruined mosques, minarets, and baths,' and that everywhere, whilst the Turks are on the decrease, Greeks, Armenians, and Jews are increasing in numbers,* is more significant than all reasoning or the partial accounts of travellers. To use again the words of Lord Carlisle:—' On the continent, in the islands, it is the Greek peasant who works and thrives; the Turk reclines, smokes his pipe, and decays. The Greek village increases its population, and teems with children; in the Turkish village you find roofless walls and crumbling mosques.' †

* Turkey and its Destiny, by Charles McFarlane. Vol. II. p. 63.
† Diary in Turkish Waters, p. 183.

So that no fate can be so afflictive, no injury to this country so great, as that which we aim at, 'the maintenance of the integrity of Turkey;' for if we repress the growth of the Christian races—if, in the words of Mr Senior, 'You leave the Turk to himself, this country, if it does not become another Greece, " by shaking off the Turkish yoke," will become another Morocco.' *

In this consists the hopelessness of expecting any improvement, so long as the Government of the Sultan continues. The evil of the present state of things arises not so much from Turkish character as from Turkish rule. This fact is sometimes contested by those who endeavour to defend the Government of that country at the expense of the people. According to their view of the case, it is the people of Turkey as contradistinguished from the Government who are the source of all the misrule, all the corruption, all the evil which have destroyed the national life; it is the people alone, according to some, who are responsible for 'the horrid massacres and outrages' by which the Turks have attempted to reduce the Christian population. The assertion, however, that these deplorable events have their origin in the spontaneous fanaticism of the people

* Senior, pp. 208, 209.

is not true. Almost every massacre which has shocked Europe has been the deliberate work of the Sultan, and has not arisen from the people of Turkey. The people have, indeed, been incited to act, and have been but too ready to obey the suggestions or directions of the Court of Constantinople; but the evidence is too complete on this matter to leave us in any doubt about the quarter from whence the instigation came. From the massacre of Scopia,* down to that of Damascus,† we have invariably seen fanatical populaces acting under the direction of their pashas, and these, again, only obeying the wishes of the Sultan and his advisers. There can be no doubt of the fact. It is this circumstance, that these were all Government massacres, ordered for the political object of keeping down the increase of the Christian population, which has led those who are best acquainted with Turkish politics to predict that there will be no more massacres on a large scale, until the Ministers of the Porte shall have recovered from the alarm felt throughout all the departments of State in Turkey, lest the recent French occupation of Syria should be permanent.

* Turkey and its Destiny, by Charles McFarlane. Vol. I. pp. 202—228.
† See the Blue Books on the Syrian Massacres, *passim*.

One consul expressly says that 'the popular fanaticism never breaks out until the fanatical tendency of the Governor is visible.'* But even then it does not break out of itself. It watches and waits for the orders of the central Government, as it did in Bulgaria. Let us follow for a moment the course of one of these massacres, one in which the evidence is complete—its beginning, its course, and conclusion. In the Syrian massacre the arms of the Christians were first taken away by the Lieutenant of the Sultan, and given to the Druse chieftains. The Christians were next led to abandon their strong positions, and to rely upon the protection of the Turkish troops. When in a safe place, the approach to their retreat was thrown open by the Turkish commander to the Druses; and the Turkish soldiers, pretending to aim at the assailants of the Christians, poured in their whole fire upon the unarmed peasants, men, women, and children. For his share in these deeds, Kurschid Pasha was sent to Rhodes, where he soon became 'the fountain of all honour and advancement' † in that island. Tahir Pasha,

* Report of Consuls on Condition of Christians in Turkey, p. 28.
† Mr Gregory's Speech in the House of Commons, May 29, 1863.

who presided at the massacre, was allowed to retire to Beyrout,* whilst the guilty agent in the Jeddah massacre, Namik Pasha, was first rewarded with the office of Minister at War, and then appointed Pasha of Bagdad. We seem in this to be reading the history of the Bulgarian atrocities. Turkish rule is invariable.

In considerations of general policy, in those deeper matters which involve the life of a nation, too great stress is oftentimes laid upon mere material interests. All is not to be settled by appeals to

* 'When I was in Syria in the spring of 1861, I inquired what had become of Tahir Pasha, whom I had known at Kars. I was told that he had been adjudged worthy of death by the almost unanimous verdict of the European commission, for having presided over and directed the wholesale massacres of Christian villages of unresisting and disarmed men, women, and children. This man had received an English education, having been for six years at the Woolwich Artillery School. His sentence had been commuted to imprisonment for life, and so I concluded he was incarcerated in a gloomy dungeon.

Before I left Beyrout, I was admiring the position of a building placed so as to command the finest scenery. I saw, on the balcony, two Turks of rank playing at dominoes, and enjoying themselves in true Turkish fashion. I thought I recognized Tahir Pasha in one of them, but to make sure, I rode up to the balcony and called him by name. He came forward, and we had some conversation together.'—*Extract of a Letter from Dr Sandwith.*

tables of exports and imports. There are more enduring interests than can be represented by bales of cotton goods and crates of earthenware. Communities of slave-owners may be larger importers of dry goods than a like number of freemen. Accident may cause this. The former may be larger purchasers merely because they are smaller producers. We are not, however, to make bills of lading the only measure of our sympathies, nor pore curiously over the columns of exports and imports, before we determine whether slavery be evil; whether despotism be preferable to constitutionalism; whether a profligate Mussulman Government shall so far enlist our support as to make us indifferent to the condition of the millions of Christians pining under its yoke. For this reason I should not have thought of appealing to the figures of the Custom-house. But I am willing to meet the friends of the Turkish Government on this ground. It is not that which I should have chosen, but it yields no support to those who cry out for the preservation of 'the integrity of Turkey,' in order that Manchester goods may not hang heavily upon our hands. I have abundantly proved, from the testimony of every one who has written on Turkey, that the race is dying out in every province of the empire, whilst the Christians

on the same soil are uniformly increasing in numbers. Now, under these circumstances, we should expect to find some fluctuation in the value of the exports and imports to that country. If the declining, or Mussulman, race, were in the main the chief purchasers or producers, then we should find the exports and imports suffer a corresponding diminution. If, however, the increasing race, the Christian subjects of Turkey, are the better customers for the produce of the rest of the world, then the imports will show an increase proportionate to that of the increase of this part of the population. Now we were told by Mr Layard, in his zealous defence of Turkey some years ago, that—
'In 1831 the Turkish import trade from England amounted to £888,684; and in 1839 it had increased to £1,430,224; in 1848 to £3,116,365; and in 1860 to £5,639,898. The export trade had increased no less rapidly from £1,387,416 in 1840, to £3,202,558 in 1856, and £5,505,492 in 1860, the Danubian Principalities included. In fact, the trade with England had increased in twenty-three years 635 per cent. The results as regards France have been no less remarkable. In 1833 the imports from that country amounted in value to 16,730,000 francs; in 1856 they had risen to

91,860,000 francs. The exports in 1833 were only 874,000 francs; in 1856 they had risen to 131,546,258 francs. The revenue of Turkey shows a no less extraordinary result. In the time of Sultan Mahmoud it amounted to only £3,000,000 a year; in 1850 it had risen to £7,000,000: it has now reached £15,000,000.' *

How much of this increase is due to the freedom of the Danubian Principalities; how much of this must be credited to Servia, Wallachia, and Moldavia, Mr Layard did not tell us: though it is noteworthy, that in order to show this great increase, he has to include countries now free from the Ottoman yoke, and flourishing because free.

But in culling these figures, Mr Layard unaccountably overlooked others which are still more deeply significant of the difference between the slumberous and decaying Turkish race and the active and advancing Greek people. Thirty years ago, Greece commenced its national life. Till that time it was a province of Turkey. It has now a population of only about 1,200,000—just a twentieth part of the population of Turkey. Yet the return of the

* The Condition of Turkey and her Dependencies. A Speech delivered in the House of Commons, May 29, 1863, by A. H. Layard, Esq. M.P. (Murray), p. 57.

TURKISH PROMISES AND NON-PERFORMANCES. 195

ships and tonnage entering the port of Constantinople in the years 1857 and 1861, gives us these remarkable items :—

	1857.		1861.	
	Ships.	Tons.	Ships.	Tons.
Turkish . .	4,055	377,500	3,690	360,612
Greek . .	2,738	461,957	3,210	527,131
Ionian Islands	290	45,634	500	82,853

So that the whole shipping, coastwise and foreign, sailing under the Turkish flag, and entering the port of its own capital, is less than that of the petty kingdom of Greece, and the former is declining, whilst the latter is increasing.*

One fact, however, is clear from the figures which I have just given. With the rapid decline of the Turkish race the foreign trade as rapidly increases, whilst the increase in trade keeps pace with the increase in the numbers, the activity, and the intellectual progress of the subject races. What, then, is the inference, the only inference to be drawn from these facts, but that the Turks are neither consumers of foreign goods, nor producers of articles of commerce to any appreciable amount; and that,

* Statistical Tables of Trade of Foreign Countries. 'Parliamentary Papers.'

when the whole race has disappeared from the countries which it occupies, indeed, but does not fill; which it possesses but only to render desolate and to curse with sterility; that then, not merely will the peace of the rest of the world be less frequently menaced, but its commerce will be largely augmented.

Increasing wealth implies industrious population; it does not prove that they are not oppressed. Tyrants tire of persecuting when there is unyielding submission, and no element exists to alarm their fears. Even the Turk would not plunder, unless stimulated by the knowledge of the gains of industry hoarded up or invested by the Christian races. But increase in numbers, and even augmenting wealth, is no evidence that the people are not oppressed. History gives us many examples of great increase in numbers, in wealth, and in intelligence, in face of grievous tyranny, and in defiance of cruelties resorted to to keep down the advance of a subject race. It was the growth of the Low Countries, in population and material resources, which, awakening the alarm of Spain, led to their oppression. The Prime Minister of Philip the Second retorted the charge of cruelty and wrong by pointing to the growth of Leyden and the thriving commerce of Antwerp. His Under Secretary for Foreign Affairs praised the tolerant rule of Alva, and condemned the restlessness and ingratitude of the Hollanders, much as an official now eulogized Turkish Pashas and condemned the discontented Christians; and all the members of the Spanish Cabinet united in attributing the movements in the Low Countries to 'foreign intrigues,' and to 'persons of various kinds not identified with or belonging to the native population.' *

Be it remembered, then, that these massacres are not the spontaneous outbreaks of Mussulman fanaticism directed against Christians, nor cruelties springing from the rapacity of the Turkish Government, and aimed against its richer subjects merely. It is the oppression of self-preservation springing from the alarm felt by the Turks at the increasing numbers, wealth, and influence of the Christians, and at their growth, notwithstanding all the cruel means which have been resorted to in order to keep down the increase of the Christian population. History is ever repeating itself. We may see in Turkey the same spectacle which the rulers of Rome beheld in the early centuries of the Christian era, the growth within the empire of a despised and persecuted sect; growing, though persecuted—nay, as it seemed,

* Sir Henry Bulwer's Circular to Her Majesty's Consuls in the Ottoman dominions.

growing because persecuted. But not only in this particular have we a parallel between the condition of the early Christians and those of modern times in countries subjected to Turkish rule, we have a repetition, also, of the means which the Neros and the Diocletians attempted to prevent the growth of the people and to destroy the hostile religion. But we may find a closer parallel than even this. When I read of the oppression which is the normal condition of the Christians of Turkey; when I think of the massacres of Damascus and Jeddah, I am reminded of the hard bondage of the Jews and the instincts of Pharaoh; and in a few verses in the beginning of the book of Exodus I read a faithful picture of the growth of the Christian people amidst oppression, and of the cruel policy by which the government of Turkey endeavours to restrain the increase of a race which it hates and fears:—'And the children of Israel were fruitful, and increased abundantly, and multiplied, and waxed exceeding mighty; and the land was filled with them. Now there arose up a new king over Egypt. . . . And he said unto his people, Behold, the people of the children of Israel are more and mightier than we: Come on, let us deal wisely with them; lest they multiply, and it come to pass, that, when there falleth out any war, they join also unto our enemies, and fight against us, and so get them up out of the land. Therefore they did set over them taskmasters to afflict them with their burdens. . . . But the more they afflicted them, the more they multiplied and grew. And they were grieved because of the children of Israel. And the Egyptians made the children of Israel to serve with rigour: And they made their lives bitter with hard bondage, in mortar, and in brick, and in all manner of service in the field: all their service, wherein they made them serve, was with rigour.'* And when hard bondage failed to thin their numbers sufficiently, and to stay the increase of the oppressed people, then we read that Pharaoh ordered the destruction of the male children, from state policy, just as now, from the same state policy, the Sultan, from time to time, directs the massacre of his Christian subjects.

But it is not the fact of the oppression and wrong practised throughout the Turkish empire which, as an Englishman, I chiefly regret; it is that, in defiance of all our boasted sympathy with enslaved and suffering people, in defiance of all our traditions of non-intervention in the internal affairs of other countries, we strengthen by our influence and our

* Exodus i. 7—14.

material power the hands of the oppressor, and are continually meddling, against this suffering people, in the internal government of Turkey. The impression that we do so is increasing throughout the dominions of the Sultan. This knowledge is embittering the people, unhappily subject to his rule, against England. It is acting also as a perpetual irritant to France and Russia; excusing, and, as they think, rendering necessary, their interference, and sowing the seeds of future trouble and wars between the Great Powers of Europe. At least half our warlike preparations and expenses of late years have arisen from this one source. The impression that we so interfere is, indeed, not groundless; it is avowed by Ministers of State, and recorded in official documents. 'Her Majesty's Government wishes, as you well know, to maintain the Ottoman Empire,' is the language of diplomacy; but it does far more than wish; in order to accomplish this object it tramples on all other considerations, it disregards every right, and tolerates the breach of every treaty which has been made for the amelioration of the people of this 'Ottoman Empire.'

CHAPTER VI.

THE REVOLT OF THE HERZEGOVINA.

THE vilayet of Bosnia, including the Herzegovina, has been among the most misgoverned of all the provinces of European Turkey. The peculiarity of its population, a Mahometan aristocracy, at once tyrannous towards the Christian rayahs and turbulent in their relations to Constantinople; an active minority of Latin Christians, due in a great measure to the fostering protection of Austria, and invested with exclusive privileges from the Porte, and hostile, from connection with Rome, to any national sentiment, has added largely to the element of mischief which exists in other provinces. Hence the language of Prince Gortschakoff in 1860, who, speaking of 'the increasing serious condition of the Christian provinces under the rule of the Porte,' adds, that he refers 'especially to Bosnia, Herzegovina, and Bulgaria.' *

Omitting all mention of Bulgaria, beyond noting the significancy of this warning, and confining my remarks to the state of Herzegovina when the insurrection of 1875 first broke out, I find Mr Holmes, the English Consul in Bosnia, writing and saying that 'in the Herzegovina there is much more oppression to complain of' † than in Bosnia. The sterile soil, the small extent of fruitful land, the exorbitant taxation, added much to the evils intolerable in other parts. On this Mr Evans bears testimony: 'The case of Herzegovina differs in many respects from that of their Bosnian brothers. This is due to the difference in the physical condition of the two countries. In Bosnia there are many tracts, like the Possavina, of marvellous fertility, where the most extortionate Government cannot so entirely consume the fatness of the land, as not to leave the rayah considerable gleanings. Far otherwise is the case in the Herzegovina. The greater part of this country may be briefly described as a limestone desert, and it is the terrible poverty of the soil which makes the

* See ante, p. 12.
† Correspondence respecting Affairs in Bosnia and Herzegovina, p. 29.

position of its Christian tiller so unendurable.'*
This desert was made more barren by the policy of
the Turkish Government. A few years before it had
inflicted an injury upon the country by the destruction of the forests, which covered a soil hardly fitted
for any purpose save that of the growth of timber.
The fertility of much of this country was seriously
impaired by this destruction, and the peasantry were
the chief sufferers. I have elsewhere described the
scene of the gigantic fire which raged for many months
in South Herzegovina. Writing at the time, I said:—
'Three or four miles' ride from Ostrug brought us
to the northern frontier of Montenegro at Gradatz,
and gave me a spectacle which I hope, for the sake
of our common humanity, cannot be paralleled in any
part of the world. We pulled up our horses at the
edge of a precipitous slope, and looked down upon
the beautiful plain of Niksich in the Herzegovina,
clothed in perennial green and interlaced by two or
three small streams of water. To the north this
plain is backed by a range of mountains—the true
geographical frontier of Montenegro, but at present
in the occupation of the Turks. This range was
formerly wooded, and even yet remains of noble

* Through Bosnia and Herzegovina, p. 329.

forests in some parts blacken the slope of the limestone mountains. When we looked at it, however, the whole range was almost concealed by dense clouds of smoke. For eighteen months these mountains have been burning, and the magnificent oaks and beeches which furnished the country around with the choicest timber are now almost wholly destroyed. This has been done by orders from Constantinople, in order to form a sterile frontier, but its effect will be to destroy the plain which lies at the foot of the mountains, and to reduce it to the condition of the arid plains of Albania on the other frontier of Montenegro. But it will do more than even this: it will diminish the tributaries of the Zeta which flow through Montenegro, and render barren much of the scanty territory possessed by these people. Such a flagrant injury to the country of a neighbour is surely contrary to the spirit if not to the letter of the law of nations, and now the Turk has been brought within the pale of civilization such an act merits our strongest reprobation.' *

This piece of vandalism, of stupid wanton destruction, was not without some influence upon the outbreak of last year. With diminished fertility the

* Good Words, September, 1866.

taxes were extorted as before. It was only the helpless who was to suffer from the waste caused by the Government of Turkey, and all trustworthy accounts represent the outbreak as occasioned by the exaction of the farmers of taxes. Lord Derby, writing on July 29, 1875, and speaking of the troubles in the Herzegovina, says that 'the rising, in the opinion of the Austro-Hungarian Government, had its origin in discontent arising from financial causes.'* And Mr Consul Holmes tells us that 'discontent undoubtedly exists against *most* of the chief Turkish landowners, and against the Zapatiehs and tax-farmers.' † But on this point we are able to cite the Porte itself as a witness. 'The first Secretary of His Majesty the Sultan,' writing to the Grand Vizier, and speaking of the prospect of putting down the insurrection, says: 'Although there is every reason to hope that, thanks to the measures to be taken, the proposed object will be completely achieved, it is not the less true that the causes which produce trouble among the peaceable populations are in a great measure due to the unseemly conduct of some incapable functionaries, and particularly to the exactions to which the avaricious farmers of taxes bind themselves in the hope of a

* Correspondence, &c., p. 3.
† Ibid. p. 29.

larger profit.'* With this evidence before us the words of Count Von Bothman, the German consul, are sadly significant: 'God only knows what the rayahs suffer in the country districts.' God indeed only knows, no words of man can describe them, hardly can the imagination of man picture them.

The testimony of Lord Derby that the insurrection was due to 'financial causes,' which in plain English means extortion by the tax-gatherers, and not to 'Russian agents,' is borne out by the report of a foreign consul which appeared in the 'Times.' He says: 'There were no foreign influences which caused the movements, but cases of unusual maladministration.' † On this Mr Evans remarks: 'The most galling oppression, and the main cause of the present revolt, is to be found in the system and manner of taxation. The centralized government set up in Bosnia since 1851 is so much machinery for wringing the uttermost farthing out of the unhappy Bosniac rayah. The desperate efforts of Turkish financiers, on the eve of national bankruptcy, have at last made the burden of taxation more than even the long-suffering Bosniac can bear. It was the last straw.

* Correspondence, &c., p. 17.
† 'Times,' December 15, 1875.

'The principal tax—besides the house and land-tax, and that paid by the "Christian" in lieu of military service, which is wrung from the poorest rayah for every male of his family down to the baby in arms—is the Eighth, or, as it is facetiously called by the tax-collector, the tenth, which is levied on all the produce of the earth. With regard to the exaction of this tax, every conceivable iniquity is practised. To begin with, its collection is farmed out to middle men, and these, *ex-officio* pitiless, are usually by origin the scum of the Levant. The Osmanli or the Sclavonic Mahometan possesses a natural dignity and self-respect which disinclines him from such dirty work. The men who come forward and offer the highest price for the licence for extortion are more often Christians—Favourite Greeks—adventurers from Stamboul, members of a race perhaps the vilest of mankind. No consideration of honour, or religion, or humanity, restrain these wretches. Having acquired the right to farm the taxes of a given district, the Turkish officials and gendarmerie are bound to support them in wringing the uttermost farthing out of the *misera contribuens plebs*. And it is natural that this help should be most readily forthcoming when needed to break the resistance of the rayah.

'These men time their visitation well. They appear in the villages before the harvest is gathered, and assess the value of the crops according to the present prices, which of course are far higher just before the harvest than after it. But the rayah would be well contented if their exactors stopped here. They possess, however, a terrible lever for putting the screw on the miserable tiller. The harvest may not be gathered till the tax, which is pitilessly levied in cash, has been extorted. If the full amount—and they often double or treble the legal sum—is not forthcoming, the tax-gatherer simply has to say, "Then your harvest shall rot on the ground till you pay it," and the rayah must see the produce of his toil lost, or pay a ruinous imposition which more than swamps his profits. Or if he remains obstinate, there are other paraphernalia of torture worthy of the vaults of the Inquisition. A village will occasionally bind together to defend themselves from the extortioners. Thereupon the tithe-farmer applies to the civil power, protesting that if he does not get the full amount from the village, he will be unable in his turn to pay the Government. The Zaptiehs, the factotums of the Turkish officials, are immediately quartered on the village, and live in them, insult their wives and ill-treat their children.

With the aid of these gentry all kinds of personal tortures are applied to the recalcitrant. In the heat of summer men are stripped naked and tied to a tree smeared over with honey or other sweet stuff, and left to the tender mercies of the insect world. For winter extortion it is found convenient to bind people to stakes, and leave them barefooted to be frost-bitten; or at other times they are shoved into a pig-sty and cold water poured on them. A favourite plan is to drive a party of rayahs up a tree or into a chamber, and then smoke them with green wood. Instances are recorded of Bosniac peasants being buried up to their heads in earth, and left to repent at leisure.' *

Under such a state of things it is little wonder that the peasants of Herzegovina are discontented with a Government which exacts its taxes by these means. He has little less reason to be contented with his Mussulman landlord. Again I borrow from the pages of the same volume, the most recent and, so far as my testimony is of value, the most truthful account which has been published of this down-trodden district. 'The Christian *kmet*, or tiller of the soil, is worse off than many a serf in our

* Through Bosnia and Herzegovina, 256—258.

darkest ages, and lies as completely at the mercy of the Mahometan owner of the soil as if he were a slave. Legally ... the Bey or Aga can break the law with impunity. He is thus allowed to treat his *kmet* as a mere chattel; "he uses a stick and beats the *kmet* without pity, in a manner that no one else would use a beast." Any land that the rayah may acquire, any house he may have built, any patch of garden that his industry may have cleared among the rocks, the Aga seizes at his pleasure. The ordinary dues, as paid by the *kmet* to the landowner, as specified in the appeal of the Herzegovinian rayahs, are heavy enough. He has to pay a fourth part of the produce of the ground; to present him with one animal yearly, and a certain quantity of butter and cheese; to carry for him so many loads of wood, and if the Aga is building a house to carry the materials for it; to work for him gratuitously whenever he pleases; and sometimes the Aga requisitions one of the *kmet's* children, who must serve him for nothing; to make a separate plantation of tobacco, cultivate it, and finally warehouse the produce in his master's store; and to plough and sow so many acres of land, the harvest of which he must also carry to his master's barn. Finally, to lodge the Aga in his own house when required, and to provide for his household and dogs.' * These being the relations of the peasant to his landlord, it is not surprising that Mr Holmes should remark that 'discontent undoubtedly exists against *most* of the chief Turkish landowners,' † since the picture which Mr Evans draws of the oppression of landlords is normal in its occurrence.

Here we have the simple, all-sufficient cause of the outbreak in the Herzegovina. Apart from acts of brutal atrocity and murder which were of constant occurrence, the oppression of the Government which permitted the tax-gatherers to seize or spoil forty per cent. of the produce of the peasant's toil, and the rapacity of the landlords which took from him always twenty-five per cent. besides over-spoliation, never leaving the unhappy labourer more than one-fourth of his earnings, drove these 'peaceable populations,' ‡ as the chief secretary of the Sultan admits them to be, into open revolt. This revolt, according to the testimony of the Austro-Hungarian Government, never disposed to judge too favourably of the Sclaves, had 'its origin in discontent arising from financial causes,' and Lord Derby himself said, on the 29th July, 1875, that so far from

* Through Bosnia and Herzegovina, p. 331.
† Correspondence in Turkey, 2, p. 29.   ‡ Ibid. p. 17.

being the work of Serb agitators, that it 'is not likely to find sympathy among Austrian or Montenegrin subjects.' *

Consistent with the strictly Agrarian character of the insurrection were the demands which the peasants when driven to revolt made upon the Government of Turkey. Mr Holmes, notwithstanding his undisguised Turkish leanings, says: 'The people of Herzegovina ... only ask to remain subjects of the Sultan, with reformed laws, and a proper and just administration of them. How to secure this is the difficulty.' † Or, again: 'The chief of the insurgents demand an European intervention, and an armistice to allow them to consult and assemble at any place which might be fixed to discuss their affairs. They do not and never have desired independence or annexation to Montenegro, but they wish to remain Turkish subjects under very extensive administration reforms, the execution of which to be guaranteed by Europe.' ‡

And yet in face of these declarations of the Turkish authorities, of the Austro-Hungarian Government, of independent English travellers, and of Mr Holmes himself, we find that gentleman turning

* Correspondence in Turkey, 2, p. 5.
† Ibid. p. 23. ‡ Ibid. p. 29.

round and denying his own words, and afterwards attributing the outbreak to 'Servian agitators,' or, like Mr Baring, to 'Russian agents.' As though peasants, when exorbitant and illegal taxes were wrung from them by the Government by tying them in summer time to trees smeared with honey to be tortured by insects—as though peasants, who were bound barefooted to a stake in winter, were scorched with fire from green wood in an apartment without a chimney, or were buried to the neck in the earth, and were doomed to see their infants tossed like garbage into the stream and drowned, to witness their sons murdered with impunity, and their wives and daughters outraged without redress, needed the stimulus of 'Servian agitators,' of 'Russian agents,' or of the emissaries of 'secret societies.' Out upon such childish babble, such silly fictions. 'Agitators' I grant there were, 'agents' I admit did instigate these people to rebellion, a 'society' there was which stirred up the people to discontent, but agitators, agents, and secret societies met and conspired in one place—the Seraglio at Constantinople.

The best answer to such an idle, silly assertion is to put on record the demand of these people. Never yet did political agitators suggest so modest a list of requests. These were—

'1. That Christian girls and women should no longer be molested by the Turks.

2. That their churches should no longer be desecrated, and that free exercise of their religion should be accorded to them.

3. That they should have equal rights with the Turks before the law.

4. That they should be protected from the violence of the Zaptiehs.

5. That the tithe-farmers should take no more than they were legally entitled to, and that they should take it in due time.

To these five two were subsequently added.

6. That every house should pay in all only one ducat a year.

7. That no forced labour, either personal or by horses, should be demanded by the Government; but that labour, when needed, should be paid for, as was the case all over the world.'

These modest demands the Turkish authorities refused to listen to, unless the peasants would first give up their arms. This they were willing to do provided the Mussulman population was at the same time disarmed. In the face of Syrian and of Bulgarian, and of twenty other massacres which had followed upon the giving up of arms, this request must be pronounced a reasonable one. It was refused, and the rebellion, justifiable as it must be pronounced, went on its course, and the Bosnian insurrection, the Bulgarian massacre, and the generous attempt of Servia to interpose by arms between the Porte and its victims, were the consequences.

CHAPTER VII.

MORAL CONSEQUENCES OF THE TURKISH ALLIANCE.

It is some extenuation of a wrong that it was thoughtlessly inflicted. But even in that case the wrong-doer is bound to make some amends for the injury which has followed upon his thoughtlessness. And the thoughtlessness which we have manifested in the desire to maintain the integrity of Turkey has been the cause of much evil to the races subject to the rule of 'our faithful ally.'

In 1840-41, in pursuance of the policy of this country, by the aid of a British fleet and land forces, the Pasha of Egypt was driven from Syria, and that country was restored to the immediate rule of the Porte. I am not concerned with the policy itself which led to this. It may or may not, for aught I know, have been, on the whole, a sound policy. The state of Syria, however, at the moment when we transferred it to the hands of the Sultan, is worth noticing. The condition of that country was this:—the people were, for the first time for a century at least, enjoying security of life and property, the laws were firmly and impartially administered, crime had diminished, outrages against the Christians had almost entirely ceased; trade had revived, lands which had long gone out of cultivation were again under tillage. The change from its former misgovernment was, according to trustworthy accounts, marvellous. We interfered; we drove out the Egyptians; we transferred it to the rule of its old masters without, unhappily, making one stipulation in favour of the inhabitants. Immediately, as if by an enchanter's wand, all life died out, the lands which had been but just rescued from the desert again went out of cultivation, the old insecurity made itself felt; again we find the old outrages, the former crimes. But over and above this, the massacres which have taken place since that moment, such as Mr Rogers, Mr Cyril Graham, Mr Moore, speak of, have caused a destruction of far more than 50,000 persons, men, women, and children. This has been the result, the consequence, of our policy. It was a result which we were bound to have guarded against; which we might have foreseen. It was a crime against humanity to have handed over the people of Syria to the rule of the Porte, without some stipulation for their better treatment, some precautions against their destruction. Though it be true that

> 'Evil is wrought by want of thought,
> As well as want of heart,' *

still evil is not the less evil whatever the source may be from which it springs. But granted that this was a thoughtless wrong, we 'maintain the integrity of Turkey' in ways which lack even this extenuation, unsatisfactory as it is.

We are losing our own reputation. In our zeal to maintain the corrupt and cruel government of the Seraglio we are not really striving to maintain Turkey, for this means the Turkish people, nor the integrity of 'Turkish territory,' for this is not menaced. No European power is seeking to obtain any portion of this territory. The utmost that is asked is that 'Turkish territory' be left to the peaceable possession of the people of Turkey: that is, as I have shown, the Christian races who live in Turkey. These are the only power whom we can maintain. How this zeal for the Court, or Serag-

* Hood.

CONSEQUENCES OF TURKISH ALLIANCE. 219

lio, at Constantinople is impairing our own credit and tarnishing our own flag may be illustrated from two examples. Alas! there are abundant other instances. I will, however, only cite two on this painful topic. One shall be given as it stands in my original pamphlet, one I take from the Blue Book (Turkey, No. 2), recently issued.

At the close of the Crimean War, the Great Powers of Europe, commiserating the condition of the people of Montenegro, appointed a commission to settle certain questions of boundary which had arisen between them and the Turks. Amongst the commissioners sent from England was a military officer who was or had been consul at Bosna Serai. He and the rest of the members of the commission were hospitably received by the people of Montenegro, who entered warmly into the pacific errand on which they had come. In order to arrange the question of frontier, the commissioners traversed Montenegro; they penetrated its defiles; they made themselves familiar with its fastnesses; those gorges which had enabled its inhabitants for so many ages to defy the Turks and to defend their independence. Hardly had the commission completed their labours when war broke out between Turkey and Montenegro— between the few thousands of those sons of the

Black Mountain and the empire of 30,000,000 inhabitants. Then comes a story which is scarcely credible. No sooner had this taken place, whilst the Turkish army was preparing to invade Montenegro, the commissioner was directed by the British Government to proceed to the head-quarters of Omer Pasha, and, with the knowledge of the defiles and approaches to the Black Mountain thus obtained in peace, to place himself at the service of the Turkish general. What follows I prefer to state in the language of the correspondent of the *Times*, who dates his letter from 'Scutari,' in Albania, on the 31st of August, 1862, and who, after pointing out the defects in the organization of the Turkish army, says:—'The fault must lie therefore somewhere else. The first thing which occurs in this respect, is of course the imperfect organization of the Turkish army in all the special services, such as staff, engineering, &c. It is nothing better off in this respect than it was in the beginning of the Eastern War; nay, if possible, it is worse off, for then there was still a number of foreigners there who knew something about such things, but these have been for the most part shelved or eliminated, and now here with the flower of the Turkish army, there is not a single man who can be trusted with making even a simple sketch of the ground. How correct this is may be judged from the circumstance that the only reliable sketches of the ground which are used are due to the exertions of Mr Churchill, *Her Majesty's Commissioner in these parts. Were it not for his sketches and personal knowledge of the country, they would be working altogether in the dark. They have not a single guide who knows anything about the country, or a single spy to give them information of the movements of the mountaineers.*'

The truth of this statement has never been questioned. It has remained since the date of this letter unchallenged. It would be hard to say what law was not broken by this act. The first principles of international law were utterly disregarded. Montenegro was an independent state, and we had no right to interfere in this manner in a war in which we had no concern. And then we talk of 'Russian agents,' and of 'foreign intrigues.' If it be by means such as these that we are to 'maintain the integrity of Turkey,' it is time that we should look to our own integrity.

The second case to which I refer may be found recorded in the Blue Book recently issued.* On August 24, 1875, Sir Henry Elliott, in a letter dated from Therapia, directed Mr Holmes, consul in Bosnia, to invite the insurgent chiefs in Herzegovina

* Correspondence in Bosnia and Herzegovina, 1876.

to a conference, in order that their demands might be laid before the Sultan. He was told to represent himself as an agent of a friendly Government, to assure them that her Majesty's Government would use its influence in recommending that the legitimate grievances which might be established should be remedied or removed. He was bidden 'to urge the insurgents to avoid attacking the imperial troops during the progress of the negotiations.'* In a letter dated Sept. 1, Lord Derby approves of this course, and bids Mr Holmes 'to induce the insurgents in Herzegovina to suspend hostilities and lay their complaints before a Turkish commission.'† These chiefs at first demurred to meet the English consul, from a fear that advantage would be taken by the Turks of this meeting. At length, on the strength of British promises, they consented to meet Mr Holmes and the other consuls. Mr Holmes told the insurgents 'that they might be sure the Turkish Government was sincere in its promises, and that the attention of Europe having been drawn to their affairs, the Government could not deceive them without serious loss of honour and damage to its own vital interests.' ‡ Still the insurgents suspected the

* Correspondence in Bosnia and Herzegovina, p. 11.
† Ibid. p. 17. ‡ Ibid. p. 28.

CONSEQUENCES OF TURKISH ALLIANCE. 223

good faith of the faithless Government of Turkey, and expressed a fear that during the conference they 'would be attacked by the Turks,' on which Mr Holmes—to use his own language—'assured them that whilst we were with them we did not think they would be molested.' Accordingly, to pursue the narrative, the insurgent chiefs said, 'that if we would go to the neighbourhood of Bilekia they would meet us there, and we should perhaps be able to see many others. They said if we went they would see us and join us.' And now what took place? Mr Holmes shall say how plighted English faith was observed. 'We left them with the intention of proceeding, if possible, to Bilekia. On the way to Stolatz, however, we met a couple of battalions, provisions, and ammunitions, proceeding in the direction from which we had come. I ordered my *cavass* to inquire of some of the soldiers in charge of the baggage where they were going. They informed me that they were going to attack the insurgents we had just left next morning before daybreak. I felt very indignant, as did my colleagues, at this attempt, as it seemed to profit by the fact of our having assembled together a certain number of insurgents to attack them when off their guard. On arriving at Stolatz, the Kaimakam also stated that an attack was to be made on the insurgents we had left, and *on my expressing my disapproval of this proceeding, he said that he did not know, that he rather thought the troops were marching to Bilekia with provisions for the garrison there.* The Governor-General had been at Stolatz, and had only left for Mortar two hours before our arrival.'

Accordingly, General Chevket Pasha, afterwards infamous for his part in the Bulgarian atrocities, by what Servar Pasha in a telegraphic dispatch to the Grand Vizier calls 'clever strategy,' fell upon the unsuspecting troops, whose leaders were away, lured by the conjoint promises of Turkey and of England, and 'completely routed' them, with a loss of '160 dead on the field of battle.' *

This scandalous act of perfidy, and the disregard of the English safe-conduct, for it was this in effect, was too much for Mr Holmes, who adds, 'On the 23rd I spoke to the Governor-General about the expedition to Trussina, and he said that Ali Pasha had not orders to attack the insurgents then, but *the affair was brought on accidentally by the insurgents attacking a convoy.* I said it might have been a very serious thing for us if it had happened one day sooner.'

The reader will note the readiness with which

* Correspondence in Bosnia and Herzegovina, p. 42.

CONSEQUENCES OF TURKISH ALLIANCE. 225

the Kaimakan and Governor-General alike lied on this occasion; but while the loss of Mr Holmes might not have been 'a very serious thing,' except to himself and family, it is a very grievous thing to know that these men who were thus surprised by 'clever strategy,' were at that moment relying on the plighted word of the English consul, and under the protection of England. And yet there is in the Blue Book not a trace of any remonstrance on the part of the English Government to the Turkish authorities for dragging down our credit for truth to a level with their own. But then we must expect to sacrifice something to maintain the integrity of Turkey!

I dare not speak more on the subject. To one who loves his country nothing can be more painful than this and similar terrible revelations. Would that we could wake up from our present delusion to see that this marsh-light which we are pursuing can never be possessed—that there is nothing to be grasped in this worse than phantom of Turkish integrity, and that, like similar adventurers, whilst straining after that which has no substantial existence, we are becoming ourselves very noisome by reason of the foul mire through which we have to struggle.

15

CONCLUSION.

WHEN, thirteen years ago, I wrote the first pages of the pamphlet which I now republish with additions, it was my intention to have made use of the official records of Servia, and to have given instances of those 'cruelties and barbarities' practised daily in Bulgaria and Bosnia, the recital of which Dr Sandwith * speaks of as curdling the blood with horror. I have, however, been unable to do so in consequence of the -length to which this record of Turkish misrule and Turkish perfidy has extended. Nor is there any necessity to make use of such evidence. Though the fact that Servia has frequently protested against these atrocities perpetrated on her frontier should be borne in mind when we hear of the war between her and the Porte being 'unprovoked,' I have, however, for want of space, not made detailed use of them. At best, the facts which are

* See at p. 9.

there treasured up, the deeds of violence there written, are but the incidents which Mr Holmes, Mr Zohrab, and other English consuls make use of in their generalizations, when they speak of the terror and discontent which reign throughout the limit of their respective consulates. I have another reason for passing by these deeply affecting documents— these wailings of young nations over the cruelties of their oppressors. English authorities, though they may not be more truthful than non-English ones, are deservedly of greater weight, inasmuch as they can be tested and examined—confronted with other witnesses, and rejected if their evidence should be undeserving of attention. Men who knew Mr Senior will place reliance on his statements. Those who have met Dr Sandwith in society will acknowledge the truthfulness of his character and the opportunities which five years of travel in that country have given him of forming a judgment on matters connected with Turkey. Men cannot well doubt about Lord Carlisle's assertions or his power of describing accurately what he had observed. Mr Cyril Graham has had more abundant means of judging as to the effect of British policy in Syria than all the members of all the cabinets which have directed the affairs of England during the last half century. And the testimony of these men is uniform. I have related only one incident upon the authority of a lady who is not English. I have cited the testimony of only one Englishman who is not alive to answer the interrogations of those who are still sceptical as to the condition of the Christians of Turkey.*

My chief authorities, however, are the reports of the various consuls throughout Turkey. It is true that these were collected for a purpose. It is true that the intention of Sir Henry Bulwer, who first collected them, was to supply materials wherewith to deny the statements of Prince Gortschakoff as to the misrule and consequent discontent in Bosnia, Herzegovina, and Bulgaria. It is true that only some of these reports have been selected by the Foreign Office; that of those selected many have been pruned and mutilated—given not *in extenso*, but only in fragments—in such a way as to remind us of the famous Affghanistan despatches. Yet, garbled as the statements are—manipulated as the reports have been, there is enough remaining in that one Parliamentary Paper to demonstrate the absurdity, the impotent folly, of those who still cling to the notion of 'maintaining the integrity of Turkey.'

* This was true in the year 1863.

More noteworthy, however, than the positive evidence of the corruption, the injustice, the faithlessness, the impotence of the Turkish Government, which is met with in every page of the Consular Reports, is the negative evidence of these documents —the portentous silence—the absence of any word of hope, any suggestion as to the possibility of the Turkish race ever shaking off the death torpor which presses upon it. Talk of 'maintaining the integrity of Turkey!' As well talk of 'maintaining' the life of a corpse which is being galvanized into some mocking resemblance of the motions of a living man! As well talk of keeping garbage from decay when it is seething with putrefaction and corrupting the whole atmosphere! We may take care of the burial of a corpse and cover it reverently with earth because it has once been a living creature, but to prate about keeping it alive when it is dead is the language of a madman or a fool. We are doing much the same when we talk about 'maintaining the integrity of Turkey.'

What, then, is the picture which these English writers—these English gentlemen—present to us? The witnesses whom I cite to testify as to the actual state of the lands of the Sultan, the government of that country and its millions of subjects—

are men who have travelled in Turkey, and who have described what has passed before their eyes. In the pages of their books we see an empire occupied by two races—one the exclusive possessor of all social and political privileges—the other refused the simplest rights of humanity, and shut out from even the protection of that law which their masters have established. We see in the pages of these writers that the destruction of the ruling race is going on at so rapid a rate that within a few years, about half a century at the furthest, it will have ceased to be. This fearful destruction we learn is caused by deep inbred vices of the foulest kind, which prevail in every class of Turkish society. There is no possibility of staying the hand of the self-destroyer, for throughout the Ottoman empire we have the shocking spectacle of a whole race committing suicide—grovelling in hideous vice—dying sensually, but still dying. To arrest this the efforts of the Great Powers are as impotent as those of the smallest states. The whole world combined must needs fail in such an attempt. It is beyond the scope of political alliances.

The significant proofs of this rapid waste and destruction of man are to be seen branded on the face of the whole country. Large tracts of rich and fertile soil, in which travellers only a few years ago saw with wonder the profusion of nature, and admired the fair beauty of undulating tracts of golden corn, of luxuriant olives, and of groves of mulberry-trees, are now silent as the grave; the inhabitants all dead; the trees destroyed; the once fruitful fields a sterile sandy waste. Fertile and yet barren—fertile by the bounty of its Maker, barren by the caprice, the sins, of man. The traveller, if he revisits the scenes of his former wanderings, beholds no more the pleasing prospect which half a dozen years before met his eye, but in place of it a pathless waste over which he must track his course by the cypress-trees of deserted cemeteries—silent mourners over the villages which have disappeared from the face of God's earth. In almost every city of the empire, with scarcely one exception, within the memory of man, suburbs which were then alive with inhabitants and teeming with children, have become depopulated; this quarter by the dying out of the Turks, that by the massacre of the Christians. This is the lot which has fallen on Smyrna; this has been the ruin which has blighted Damascus; this is the spectacle which may be witnessed around Ephesus; this saddens the traveller as he silently wanders through the tenantless streets of Nicæa.

Wherever the Osmanli has planted his foot there the grass grows no more—there he brings desolation.

Let us turn away from this sight, which will meet us in every province of Turkey; let us turn our eyes upon the suffering people of that empire. If kingdoms exist not for kings, still less are people sent on God's earth merely to be playthings for Turkish Pashas, and to be trafficked in by jobbing Grand Viziers. What are the people of this the fairest region of the globe enduring, whilst their masters are dying? We see throughout the length and breadth of that land, from the Danube to the Persian Gulf—from Kars to Albania, millions of men subjected to every wrong which jealous governors can devise, or the envy of their neighbours can suggest, whilst they are deprived by law of the power to make themselves heard against the violation of law. Living in perpetual fear, without any reasonable security for life, without one safeguard for the honour of their family, unarmed, by the forethought of their rulers, in the midst of a people armed with every weapon of offence, and easily moved to fanaticism, they are daily, hourly, exposed to every outrage which envy, cupidity, lust, or anger can urge, and they are exposed to the effects of these passions without possibility of defence. In such cases, if, goaded by the sense of wrong, the sufferer should make use of the rudest weapons of defence—a stone, a club—he is guilty in the eyes of his masters of a crime; and many a boy has been executed within the last few years for no other sin than the generous impulse which led him thus too fatally to guard the honour of his sister, to avenge an outrage upon his mother. Dr Sandwith, in a letter quoted by Mr Cobden in the debate of 1863 in the House of Commons, tells us that within the last two years he 'remembers a case in which a Christian, having lost many sheep from robbers, at last loaded a gun, and kept it by him. The next time the robbers came, he fired and killed one. This Christian was publicly executed for having shot a Mussulman.'* And only two years ago the Grand Vizier, in his tour to Bulgaria, ordered to instant execution a poor lad who, in defence of a companion from the foulest assault which is heard of in the laws of any civilized country, struck and killed one of the assailants. And what the Grand Vizier then did is—I will not say law, for this is too noble a term to be used to palliate such atrocities—but the practice throughout Turkey.

But be it so, we must, say men who aspire to be

* Speech of Mr Cobden in House of Commons, May 29th, 1863.

thought statesmen, 'maintain' this accursed empire, this reign of lawlessness, this institution of persecution. We must—because it is our policy. We dare not plead that it is right, that it is just, that it is in accordance with our principles, that it squares with our professions. Call it, however, what we will. It is surely impossible that a policy so barren of good fruit, so cankered with injustice, should be much longer persisted in. We cannot, if we would, 'maintain the integrity of Turkey,' by which liberal politicians mean the government of the Sultan—the rule of the handful of pashas who spoil and evil intreat the people of that country. Let us, if we must needs interfere at all, do so for Turkey itself—for the inhabitants of that fair and fertile land. If indifferent to the sufferings of our brethren, it surely becomes us to endeavour to set limits to the encroachment of the desert—to attempt to stay the desolation of those lands which their Maker and ours has enriched with all that can delight the eye or satisfy the wants of man. Honour, natural instinct, a common faith, should lead us to desire that the people who, in this fruitful cradle of nations, are fast rising to manhood, should do so with hearts beating with gratitude and affection for England, and not with the bitter feelings of hatred. Let us not thwart and repress their generous longings to tread in the same path of freedom which, by God's blessing, has led this nation of England to so much happiness and greatness; but rather let us encourage them in their efforts to emancipate themselves from the sensual and degrading despotism which presses heavily upon their necks and corrupts their moral nature. In pursuing a magnanimous policy we shall be treading in the safest path; whilst, on the other hand, we may be assured that a policy which is based upon wrong cannot prosper, and that the Nemesis which follows a nation is even more quick-footed than that which haunts the steps of an individual.

I do not propose to speak of what English policy should be. I do not believe, however, that there are any extraordinary difficulties in the way of our acting honourably, and justly, and humanely, to the people of Turkey. And in stating this opinion I am satisfied with the weighty authority of the statesman most thoroughly acquainted with the condition of Turkey, Lord Stratford de Redcliffe. It is a serious imputation upon most of our statesmen, however, that though more than fifty years have passed by since this 'Eastern Question' first rose before their eyes, they utter to-day the same helpless cry which they did half a century ago, ' *Non pos-*

sumus'—we know not what to do. And then to account for their inaction they conjure up terrible dreams of Mahometan discontent, and of possible insurrection in India, wars in Europe, and massacres of Christian subjects in Turkey. I would not undervalue danger. Those, however, who are best able to speak as to our Mussulman fellow-subjects declare that the danger of discontent in India is imaginary. Not, however, to intrude into the region of dreams and of fiction, it may be well for us to remember that the Mussulman outbreak and mutiny in India took place at the moment we had shown our friendship for, not our hostility to, the Sultan of Turkey ; that a European war has never broken out in consequence of our intervention in favour of the Christian people of Turkey, though a very bitter, and bloody, and costly war was the result of our intervention in favour of the oppressor of the Christians ; and that massacres have always taken place at the moment when the Porte believed itself safe in defying the indignation of Europe, when it thought that it could safely depend upon British arms to shield it from punishment—in a word, when English influence has been paramount at Constantinople. In the spring of this year the correspondents of the English press, writing from that city, bore uniform testimony to the fact that Russian influence had waned away, and that the power and influence of the English ambassador were again predominant, and then—let Bulgaria tell the rest.*

It is time that this pretext for a policy were at an end. The alliance is degrading England more even than it is maintaining Turkey. It is filling our history with the record of actions as base as those which we find in the chronicles of the Turks. It is making us as faithless to all high and noble instincts as the Sultan is to treaties. It is deadening our conscience to wrong. It is tainting our public men, so that they are not ashamed to disregard truth as much as a Turkish pasha does. It cannot be persisted in without the violation of every principle of a true English policy and the sacrifice of every English virtue. For surely to disregard those principles which are enshrined in our laws, and embalmed in our literature, regardless of what evil we inflict—to strike hands with the oppressor—to

* During the height of the Bulgarian massacres our Ambassador at Constantinople thus writes:—'There is at this moment among all classes, both of Turks and Christians, an enthusiasm for Great Britain, which puts her Majesty's Government in a position in this country which they have not held for many years.'—*Sir Henry Elliot to Lord Derby*, May 31st, 1876. Correspondence on the Affairs of Turkey, No. 3, p. 238.

assist the faithless masters in afflicting their slaves—to support, to our own heavy injury, the persecutor in his barbarous treatment of those whom a common humanity binds to our fortune, and ought to bind still closer to our sympathies—is injustice for which we must needs suffer—is dishonour from which we may well shrink—is wrong for which we shall have to atone.

POSTSCRIPT.

WHILST this volume was passing through the press I received a letter from Dr Thomson, for many years resident at Beyrout, and author of *The Land and the Book*. No one is more entitled to speak of Turkey, no one knows the condition of the people, both Christian and Mussulman, better than he does, and the solemn warning which he gives may well be pondered on at this crisis. I had written to him for some information, and in his letter in reply he says—
'—There is at this moment terrible danger lest these down-trodden Bulgarians should be left to the tender mercies of the Turk; and if under any plea this be done, then their condition will be far more intolerable than it was before. This sublime uprising of the English nation in their behalf will only add to the fury of their brutal enemies. Every great meeting, every resolution passed, every speech delivered, the publication of your own pamphlet, will only add to their calamities. The Turks will

avenge themselves for all this manifestation of horror and indignation in those on whose behalf it has been manifested, and every guinea you contribute to their relief will be wrested from them with savage cruelty.'

In a letter written to me a few days after the one in which this sentence occurs, Dr Thomson says— 'For England now to use her powerful influence to force back these poor sufferers under the Turk, under any form, and from any pretended necessity, will be more monstrous than the conduct of the Bashibazûks themselves. I apprehend that the great English people must speak in tones still more stern to the present holders of power, or they may find, with shame and dismay, that all their efforts have only plunged the wretched sufferers into deeper despair and more fearful calamity.'

Only in the complete independence of Bulgaria, an independence at least as complete as that of Servia, is there the least possibility of security for life and property.

www.ingramcontent.com/pod-product-compliance
Lightning Source LLC
Chambersburg PA
CBHW031747230426

43669CB00007B/517